# Solving Deer Problems

How to Keep Them Out of
the Garden, Avoid Them on the Road,
and Deal With Them Anywhere!

## Peter Loewer

**The Lyons Press**

**Guilford, Connecticut**
**An imprint of The Globe Pequot Press**

*This book is dedicated to the North American deer in hopes that it will survive the present and inspire the future of wildlife in America.*

The Lyons Press is an imprint of The Globe Pequot Press.

Printed in the United States of America

10 9 8 7 6 5 4 3 2 1

Library of Congress Cataloging-in-Publication Data is available on file.

ISBN 1-58574-672-X

# Contents

# Introduction

"When Daniel Boone goes by at night
The phantom deer arise
And all lost, wild America
Is burning in their eyes."
—Stephen Vincent Benét
*Daniel Boone* (1942)

Recently, I received a telephone call from a friend who lives in Biltmore Forest, here in Asheville, North Carolina. Biltmore Forest is a gated community that lacks gates, and for all the years I've lived in Asheville (fourteen) it has been under attack by hordes of deer.

The residents have had public meetings in which the subjects leapt from hiring bow hunters to sterilizing the bucks and opinions, both pro and con, were shouted out by homeowners; but in the end, the final solution has been left up to the individual homeowner.

"What can I do?" my friend asked. "They're attacking everything I've planted, and I swear they know that I'm a dedicated gardener and will continue to set out plants, even though I know I might lose everything! What can I do?"

"There are solutions," I answered, "but they are not always cheap, and like life in general, they work most of the time—but there are no guarantees."

"What can I do?"

So I told her a few snippets of what's in this book. I also told her that deer are really just intelligent goats who not only mirror the world around them (a world suffering from overpopulation and loss of habitat), but among all the pest animals of America seem to know just what to do to torture gardeners in particular and landowners in general.

Before I spent twenty years in Sullivan County, New York, where the deer began their attack on our first garden when it was still in the planting stage, I thought that a deer nibbling in my garden would merely be a picturesque touch.

But during that twenty years, my wife and I gardened on a small cleared area measuring a little over two acres. Our civilized parcel was the front part of thirty-three acres, surrounded by second-growth forest (but forest just the same) located between Cochecton Center and Lake Huntington in western Sullivan County, New York.

After a year spent making our house (a cross between an abandoned farmhouse and a resort hotel) livable, we sought escape from carpentry and finishing in working the land.

When the battle with red shale and red clay was close to an end (thanks to compost, lime, and more compost), we began to grow vegetables for the table and the larder.

Soon we were knee-deep in all sorts of incredible garden pests. In the insect world, they ranged from armyworms to tent caterpillars to gypsy moths to Japanese beetles and, finally, ants. In the animal world, the threats came from chipmunks, woodchucks, voles, rabbits, and deer. The deer were the worst.

Why? It seemed as though they ate everything in their path.

Whatever the season, the local deer population seemed to look upon our land as a trendy restaurant, a place meant to provide endless reserves of food for these very intelligent goats.

Instead of bowing to rising tides of anger, I decided to try a few new (to me) procedures to stop the deer in their tracks. So I asked local farmers and hunters for their advice.

Years passed. Gardens grow—and gardens come and go.

We now live in Asheville, North Carolina, protected by surrounding highways from problems with deer in the garden. But as the Wild Gardener, I'm deluged with questions about how to control deer, what products are available, what plants deer dislike, and many more.

In addition to farmers and hunters, I have also asked highway departments, experts on deer, doctors, and vets, and searched out new products on the World Wide Web.

When trying to discover which plants deer dislike, I'm reminded of the following answer provided by Joe Seals, my good garden friend from California: "After an extensive survey of gardeners in badly deer-infested areas (after a bad winter drought that forced record numbers of wild deer into urban areas), we shortened our list to the following: oleander and old brick."

One more thing: In addition to being a gardener, I'm a naturalist. The gardener in me resents the damage that deer do to gardens, while the naturalist always wants to point out that, whatever happens, it is not the fault of the deer. As Shakespeare wrote in *Julius Caesar*, "The fault, dear Brutus, is not in our stars, but in ourselves."

For we are the disturbers of the environment—we did away with the predators, we took for development the land that deer once lived upon, we did away with the small farm and opened the path to the mega-farm, and we built the highways that the deer must cross.

Let's not forget!

> *"Quarry mine, blessed am I*
> *In the luck of the chase.*
> *Comes the deer to my singing."*
> —*Navaho hunting song*

# All About Deer

## The Typical Deer

If dandelions were rare plants, everybody would want at least one in their garden. The same holds true for deer. Endangered, they would be desired by all; but in today's numbers they've become suburban pests. All thoughts of their graceful beauty are gone. Deer are now looked upon as intelligent goats, ready and willing to eat their way through your garden and landscaping.

Deer are herbivorous mammals—like cows, cud-chewers that eat vegetation and not meat. They walk upon cloven hooves, and have trotted into the heart of our culture through books such as Felix Salton's *Bambi* and the marvelous 1942 Disney movie of the same name.

For a firsthand account of a typical deer, in this case a whitetail, I talked to Dr. Leonard Lee Rue III, the author of the authoritative volume, *The Deer of North America*.

"They are," said Dr. Rue, "incredible animals worthy of our admiration." Dr. Rue explains:

Today, the three groups—whitetails, muleys, and blacktails—probably total about twenty-five million deer. That's a lot of any single kind of wildlife. Whether or not there were more deer wandering North America before the Europeans came, nobody really knows; but, from the time of man's first arrivals on this continent, deer have been important to the survival of mankind.

When you think of what deer represented—first to the existence of the American Indians and then to the first settlers—you begin to wonder if mankind could have managed without them. Venison was a dietary staple, they used deer hides for clothing, the sinews were used to sew the skins, the bones were fashioned into awls to poke holes in the leather so the sewing could commence, the hair was used as insulation when stuffed into deer-leather moccasins, the hooves were turned into glue and ornaments, and finally, the bones and antlers became tools, weapons, decorations, and religious objects.

And never forget, the settlers were far more aggressive than the Indians when it came to the deer harvest. They didn't limit their kills to personal needs but began killing deer for both meat and deerskins, with Europe as an expanding market.

"I never thought," I said, "of the professional hunters of that time. Do you have any figures as to the kills?"

"There was a gentleman," said Dr. Rue, "one Thomas Meacham of Hopkinton, in St. Lawrence County, New York, who kept exact records of his victims. When he died in 1850, he had killed 214 wolves, 77 cougars, 219 bears, and 2,550 deer. There were others, but I think he probably holds the record.

"These men were a product of their time and thought that the wealth provided by nature would go on forever," he added.

"I live about fifty miles from Jonesborough, Tennessee," I said, "and I seem to remember that, at that time, official salaries were paid in deerskins and not greenbacks."

"That's right," he said. "But remember that in 1646, Rhode Island became the first colony to pass a law protecting deer from the hunt for at least part of the year. The laws didn't always work, but at least they tried."

Dr. Rue went on to tell me that the late 1800s were the blackest period for all sorts of wildlife on the American continent, with the northeastern states hit the hardest. By the end of the nineteenth century, New Jersey had fewer than 200 deer while in Massachusetts, Vermont, and New Hampshire, deer were so scarce that just the sight of hoofprints made newspaper headlines.

Now, thanks mainly to the increased awareness of the general public, more rigid game laws, better enforcement, and migration, the pendulum is beginning to swing the other way—although both mule deer and blacktail populations have declined slightly in recent years.

"I think," said Dr. Rue, "that much of the problem is one of habitat loss. Where once there were fields and woods, there are now housing developments. Not to mention the decline of the predator: Wolves, bobcats, lynx, even bears, are effective hunters of deer. But dogs probably take a greater toll than all other predators combined.

"And let's not forget the automobile."

## *Anatomy of a Deer*

Deer are mammalian, cloven-hoofed quadrupeds. They are the only hoofed mammals that shed their antlers every year. The females are smaller and lack antlers. Deer have a lifespan of eleven to twelve years in captivity, but few ever last that long in the wild.

Deer have excellent eyesight, geared toward detecting motion. You can prove this yourself by being downwind of a deer and moving ever so slowly. They have a great sense of smell, thought to be better than a dog's, and are endowed with a sophisticated sense of taste.

But it's their hearing that should earn salutes. In the midst of a blowing breeze, with rustling leaves, buzzing bees, and a few birdcalls thrown in for good measure, step on a stick and you'll see all deer activity stop and ears go up to find the cause of the disturbance.

Deer learn the warning sounds that other animals make when danger threatens—especially birdcalls. Yet, while feeding in the front of our Cochecton home, the milk truck rumbling up the hill never got their attention. Like people, they can adapt to noises, whether loud or just persistent.

Also like people, an adult deer has thirty-two teeth. In deer, however, the teeth are distributed to aid in chewing vegetation instead of meat.

Deer can weigh up to 300 pounds (which explains why a car or a truck hitting a deer often results in a great deal of damage to both participants), but most weigh far less. And, counter to many hunters' stories, deer rarely stand above three-and-a-half feet high at the shoulder and are only about six feet long.

Whitetails breed from the middle of September to late February, with the fawns being born in early summer. There is a 200-day gestation period. At the first birthing, does usually give birth to a single fawn; in later years, as long as food is abundant, twins are common.

Deer are ruminants and, like cows, have four-chambered stomachs and chew a cud. Four-chambered stomachs are very valuable for animals on the go: This arrangement lets a deer ingest a lot of food quickly, then digest it later in a more leisurely manner.

Unlike many animals, deer amble while they eat. They take a bite of food, walk a few feet, and then nibble again. They eat twigs, branches, and bark in the winter, lush grasses and new leaves in the spring and summer (in addition to farm crops), and in the fall turn to their favorite food: acorns. I well remember the Grunds in Cochecton, who every summer fought to keep the deer from the cornfields, as the deer would often eat the stalks with the tassels, preventing formation of a good corn crop.

A deer's coat changes color according to the season. In summer they have a short, dense coat, while in winter they grow longer, hollow hairs, which provide insulation against the cold.

They are amazing creatures.

## The Varieties of Deer

There are a number of deer species in North America. They all belong to the genus *Odocoileus,* a name bestowed by Constantine Samuel Rafinesque (1783–1840), a French-American naturalist. In 1832, Rafinesque was exploring some caves in Virginia when he found the fossilized tooth of a remote ancestor of the present whitetailed deer. He probably meant to name the genus *Odontocoelus,* meaning "hollow tooth," strangely a word often used to describe the denture of lizards. Perhaps Greek was not his strong suit. The result was the genus *Odocoileus.*

All deer descend from a ten-million-year-old common ancestor from the Pliocene Period, but about a million years ago migrated across our continent and divided into three distinct species: the white-tailed deer (*O. virginianus*), the mule deer (*O. hemionus*), and the black-tailed deer (*O. hemionus columbianus*).

## The White-tailed Deer

The white-tailed deer is divided into seventeen subspecies and makes its home in all forty-eight contiguous states and a large part of Canada. According to Dr. Rue, in the mid-1600s there were some twenty million deer in North America. They were hunted by both Native Americans and settlers, and their habitats were so denuded that, by the end of the 1800s, only about fifty thousand survived.

Then conservation entered the scene, a philosophy that worked with such success that today there are again some twenty million white-tailed deer at large in the forty-eight states.

Whitetails are divided into the following subspecies:

1. Virginia whitetail (*O. virginianus virginianus*) eat their way across Virginia, West Virginia, Kentucky, Tennessee, North and South Carolina, Georgia, Alabama, and Mississippi. This moderately large deer with fairly heavy antlers has adapted to an astounding number of habitats, ranging from the Piedmont's coastal marshes, woodlands, and swamps to the tops of the Great Smoky Mountains. The Virginia whitetail also makes its home just a few miles from my city garden in Asheville, and has become a thorn in the side of western North Carolina suburbanites.

2. The northern whitetail (*O. virginianus borealis*) is the largest subspecies and the one which made

garden life so difficult in Sullivan County. This animal is found throughout New England, the mid-Atlantic states, and the upper Midwest, as well as the Canadian provinces of New Brunswick, Nova Scotia, Quebec, Ontario, and parts of Manitoba. Not bad for a subspecies!

3. The Dakota whitetail (*O. virginianus dacotensis*) is slightly smaller in stature, and in winter has a paler coat than the northern whitetail. Its range covers North and South Dakota, parts of Nebraska, Kansas, Wyoming, and Montana, and the Canadian provinces of Manitoba, Saskatchewan, and Alberta.

4. The Northwest whitetail (*O. virginianus ochrourus*) is another large deer with a cinnamon-brown winter coat. It makes its home in Montana, Idaho, Washington, Oregon, California, Nevada, Utah, and the Canadian provinces of British Columbia and Alberta.

5. The Columbian whitetail (*O. virginianus leucurus*) is presently on the endangered species list and found only in the Federal Columbian White-tailed Deer Refuge, and along the Columbia River near Cathlamet, Washington. There are presently less than 500 animals remaining.

6. The Coues or Arizona whitetail (*O. virginianus couesi*) is a small deer with large ears and tail in proportion to its body size. It lives in the desert regions of southeastern California, southern Arizona, southwestern New Mexico, and northern Mexico.

7. The Texas whitetail (*O. virginianus texanus*) is the largest of the southern deer and lives in western Texas, Oklahoma, Kansas, southeastern Colorado, eastern New Mexico, and northern Mexico.

8. The Carmen Mountains whitetail (*O. virginianus carminis*) is a large deer, though smaller than the northern whitetail, and makes its home in the Big Bend region of southern Texas, limited to the Carmen Mountains on both sides of the Rio Grande.

9. The Avery Island whitetail (*O. virginianus mcilhennyi*) is known as the deer of the Texas Big Thicket Country. It's a large deer with a brownish winter coat and a range that stretches along the Gulf Coast of Texas and Louisiana.

10. The Kansas whitetail (*O. virginianus macrourus*) is the fourth subspecies found in Texas. A large deer, it is also found in Oklahoma, Kansas, Nebraska, Iowa, Missouri, Arkansas, and Louisiana.

The following four subspecies live on islands far enough from the mainland to prevent interbreeding with one another or with mainland subspecies:

11. The Bull's Island whitetail (*O. virginianus taurinsulae*) is found only on Bull's Island of South Carolina.

12. The Hunting Island whitetail (*O. virginianus venatorius*) is another island habitant of South Carolina, found only on Hunting Island.

13. The Hilton Head Island whitetail (*O. virginianus hiltonensis*) ran across my headlights when I was on a lecture tour in Sea Island, and is another island variation.
14. The Blackbeard Island whitetail (*O. virginianus nigribarbis*) lives only on the islands of Blackbeard and Sapelo, in Georgia.
15. As you might guess from its name, the Florida whitetail (*O. virginianus seminolus*) makes its home in the Everglades.
16. The Florida coastal whitetail (*O. virginianus Osceola*) lives in the Florida panhandle region, southern Alabama, and Mississippi. It is not as large as the Florida or Virginia whitetail.
17. Finally, the smallest of them all, the Florida Key deer (*O. virginianus clavium*) is also on the endangered-species list. If ever the word "cute" applied to an animal, it's the Florida Key deer. After decades of losing its habitat to immigrants, plus the continuing problem of getting hit by cars, its population numbers only about 350.

## The Mule Deer and the Black-tailed Deer

Mule deer and blacktails live west of the Mississippi River. Muleys are often larger than whitetails, though size is not a reliable identifier. The dead giveaway is their tail: narrow, short, and tipped with black.

There are six subspecies of mule deer:

1.  The Rocky Mountain mule deer (*Odocoileus hemionus hemionus*) is the northernmost mule deer, the largest in size and weight and having the darkest colorations. Although you would expect a northern deer to have a paler coat, Dr. Rue suggests that, because this deer's habitat is forested, their coat helps them blend into their surroundings. This subspecies is found in the Canadian provinces of British Columbia, Saskatchewan, Alberta, Manitoba, and the Northwest Territories, in addition to Washington, Idaho, Montana, North and South Dakota, Minnesota, Nebraska, Wyoming, Oregon, California, Nevada, Utah, Colorado, Oklahoma, New Mexico, and Arizona.

2.  The California mule deer (*O. hemionus californicus*) lives only in California, from the Sierras to the Pacific. It's smaller than the Rocky Mountain mule deer and has a smaller white rump patch.

3.  The southern mule deer (*O. hemionus fuliginatus*) lives along the California coast, from south of Los Angeles into Mexico's Baja Peninsula. It's a dark subspecies about the size of the California mule deer.

4.  The Inyo mule deer (*O. hemionus inyoensis*) has a small range around Inyo County, California. It's of medium size, with coloring between that of the Rocky Mountain mule deer and the California mule deer.

5.  The burro deer (*O. hemionus eremicus*) lives in the southeastern corner of California and from southwestern Arizona south into Mexico. It's smaller

than the Rocky Mountain mule deer and lighter in coloration.

6.  The desert mule deer (*O. hemionus crooki*) is the kind of animal that songs should be written about. It survives in the harshest of conditions: intense heat and harsher cold, limited forage, little water, and lack of cover from enemies. Even so, this palest of the mule deer survives against all odds—but increasing whitetail populations will eventually lead to declines in the genetic stock.

The black-tailed deer represent two more subspecies:

1.  The Columbian black-tailed deer (*O. hemionus columbianus*) lives in California, Washington, Oregon, and British Columbia. It survives in a range of climates, from high mountains to dry chaparral, and makes its home in the densest and wettest forests of North America. Columbian blacktails have a redder coat than mule deers and are smaller than the average whitetail.

2.  The Sitka black-tailed deer (*O. hemionus sitkensis*) sports a cinnamon-brown coat and is smaller, on average, than the Columbian. It was originally found in the coastal rain forests, from the Queen Charlotte Islands off British Columbia to the southeastern Alaska Panhandle. But back in 1916, herds were introduced to islands in Prince William Sound and, later, to the Kodiak Islands and the Yakutat area.

# 2

# *Thoughts About Deer (and a Few Other Garden Animals)*

The following essays deal with deer from the points of view of writers and naturalists (including my own).

I begin with Henry David Thoreau, a man whom most would credit with originating America's naturalist tradition. The essay is an imaginary interview with Thoreau, written for a study on garden animals, and based on actual quotations taken from his journals (*The Journal of Henry D. Thoreau,* edited by Torrey and Allen, Dover Publications, New York, 1962).

The second essay is a conversation with Dr. Leonard Lee Rue III, one of America's most respected naturalists and wildlife photographers.

The third is a conversation with Benjamin Wechsler, a noted conservationist who has studied deer and maintained a hunting camp for many years.

The last is one of my favorite garden columns about deer, written in 1985.

## *A Conversation with Thoreau on Garden Animals*

Since the invention of *Star Trek*'s warp drive, a number of things have become possible that were impossible in times past.

For example, one day last summer Henry David Thoreau visited my garden. The mountains were seething under a late-spring Bermuda high. By nine o'clock in the morning, the mercury hit 85°F—and for our garden, that's hot.

There's a spot under an archway of bittersweet vines where the sun is filtered twice: once through a high canopy of oak leaves and once through the bittersweet. Earlier in the morning, I had put two French garden chairs there plus a small table set for tea.

We settled into place and Thoreau put his straw hat down by the side of the chair.

"Just as the sun was rising this morning," he said, "I saw a rainbow in the west horizon, and I thought of,

'Rainbow in the morning,
Sailors take warning;
Rainbow at night,
Sailor's delight.'"

"We need the rain," I said. "So if it comes, it'll be welcome."

We stirred the cups of tea.

Late the day before, while driving along the River Road, a busy two-lane highway that parallels the Swannanoa River in South Asheville, I had seen a woodchuck eating grass and clover right next to the roadside. The trucks, cars, and busses didn't bother him at all; he just kept chewing.

So I asked Thoreau about woodchucks, because I knew they were a favorite animal in his scheme of things.

## The Woodchuck

"One June morning in 1854," he said, "while rambling in the grassy hollows north of Goose Pond, where the woods never seem to grow but the grasses are in blossom around the edges, and small black cherries and sand cherries straggle down into them, I often find woodchucks. They love such places and, when disturbed, usually wabble off with that peculiar loud squeak like the sharp bark of a red squirrel, then stand erect at the entrance of their holes, ready to dive into it as soon as you approach. Are there any in your garden?"

"No," I said. "We're cut off from the open land along the river by a highway that's busy twenty-four hours a day, so a woodchuck would be unlikely to make it across the road. But I have fond memories of them from our garden in the Catskills and from walking in the woods."

"Do you remember their scientific name?"

"Yes, it's *Marmota monax*, the genus name because of the animal's resemblance to the marmot found in the Black

Hills of South Dakota. The species name is from the Delaware Indian word *monachgen*, for woodchuck. They hibernate in the winter, but not always too deeply, and are most active in the morning and late afternoon. And they can climb and swim."

"I knew they could swim, but climb?"

"When we lived in the Catskill Mountains, we surrounded a new vegetable bed with a snow-fence made of wooden slats about four feet high, and held together by twisted wire at the top, the bottom, and along the middle. One morning I watched a big chuck climb up using his claws in the wood and on the wire, until reaching the top, he jumped down and walked to the beans."

"They love beans. Back in July of 1845, I remember writing in the journal that my enemies in the garden were worms, cool days, and most of all woodchucks. They nibbled an eighth of an acre clean. I planted in faith, but they reaped. When they run they look like a ripe fruit mellowed by winter."

"I know I read in your journal about your meeting a woodchuck," I said.

"I've been very friendly with woodchucks," he said as he sipped his tea. "One April morning in 1852, I turned round the corner of Hubbard's Grove and saw a woodchuck, the first of the season. He was sitting in the middle of the field, about thirty-five feet from the fence that bounds the woods and a few hundred feet from me. I ran along the fence and cut him off, even though we both started running at the same time. When I was only about twenty feet away, he stopped, and I did the same; then he ran again, and I ran up to within three feet of him, when he stopped again.

"I squatted down and surveyed him at my leisure. His eyes were dull black with a faint chestnut iris, with but little expression and that more of resignation than of anger. The general aspect of the coarse grayish brown fur was a sort of gristle with a lighter brown next to the skin. The head of a woodchuck is between that of a squirrel and a bear, flat on the top and dark brown, and darker still or black on the tip of the nose. The whiskers are black— about two inches long—and the ears are very small and rounded, set far back and nearly buried in the fur. His feet are black with long, slender claws for digging.

"He appeared to tremble or was shivering with the cold. When I moved, he gritted his teeth quite loudly, sometimes striking the under jaw against the other chatteringly, sometimes grinding one jaw on the other, yet as if more from instinct than anger. Whichever way I turned, that's the way he headed. I took a foot-long twig and touched his snout, at which he started forward and bit the stick, lessening the distance between us to two feet, and still held his ground. I played with him tenderly awhile with the stick, trying to open its gritting jaws. Even his long incisors, two above and two below, were presented. But I thought he would go to sleep if I stayed long enough. He stood there, half sitting, half standing, and we looked at each other for about a half hour, until I swear we began to feel mesmeric influences. When I was tired, I moved away, wishing to see him run, but I could not get him started. He wouldn't stir as long as I was looking at him or could see him.

"I walked around him, but he turned as fast and continued to front me. So I sat down by his side within a foot. I talked to him in quasi-forest lingo, a kind of baby talk, at any rate in a conciliatory tone, and thought that I had some influence on him. He gritted his teeth less. I chewed checkerberry leaves and presented them to his nose and was met with a grit. With a little stick, I lifted one of his paws to examine it, and held it up at pleasure. I turned him over to see what color he was beneath—more purely brown—though he turned himself back again sooner than I could have wished. His tail was also all brown, though not very dark, rat tail-like, with loose hairs standing out on all sides like a caterpillar brush. He really had a rather mild look. I spoke kindly to him. I reached checkerberry leaves to his mouth. If I had a few fresh bean leaves from my bean garden, I'm sure I could have tamed him completely. I finally had to leave him without seeing him move from the place.

"I respect woodchucks as one of the natives and I think I might learn some wisdom from him. His ancestors have lived here longer than mine, or yours. He is more thoroughly acclimated and naturalized than we are."

## The Eastern Chipmunk

There's a three-foot wall of field stone about ten feet away from where we sat that runs the length of the perennial border. We both saw a quick movement, a living streak of brown race along the wall, then suddenly disappear in the leaves of a spiraea bush.

"It's a chipmunk," I said. "They have tunnels behind that wall and no matter how I try to keep them away, they keep coming back. If I fill a tunnel in the morning, it's back by mid-afternoon, but I never find a hint of the soil they move."

"Neither have I. How do they do it?"

"According to Lawrence Wishner in his book *Eastern Chipmunks, Secrets of Their Solitary Lives* (Washington, D.C.: Smithsonian Institution Press, 1982), their tunnel construction is carried out with a 'working tunnel.' They push the dirt along with their noses and their feet, opening everything from below. The last thing they do is excavate the entrance tunnel, using that dirt to fill in the working tunnel. Their tunnels are, of course, complicated, and contain food storage chambers and nesting chambers lined with dry leaves. Droppings are never found in the chambers.

"And," I added, "Chipmunks are so clean they seldom have a hair out of place, and according to many observers, their almost obsessive cleanliness means they have few, if any, external parasites."

"I never had a formal garden like yours, so I wonder how much damage they do?" he mused.

"Oh, some gardeners claim chipmunks are major pests, but to me, they're some of the most intelligent creatures in the garden, with a unique social system all their own. So I don't begrudge them their holes, although I do swear a bit when I'm forced to fill them up."

"Their scientific name," said Thoreau, "is *Tamias striatus*, the genus name from the Greek word for a steward, referring either to their food-gathering capabilities or the way they run their existences. The species name, of course, refers to their striped coat. I, on occasion, called them chipmunks, but usually I called them 'striped squirrels'."

The lone chipper on the garden wall surfaced for just a moment.

"Although they are usually unsocial among themselves," I said, "I've always been delighted by their antics, especially when they put tails in air and leap from log to log or along a wall."

"In very early spring of 1855," he recounted, "I was walking along the sunny hillside on the south of Fair Haven Pond, which unfortunately the choppers had just laid bare, when I heard a rustling amid the dry leaves on the hillside and saw a striped squirrel eyeing us from its resting place on the bare ground. It sat there until we were within some fifteen feet, then suddenly dived into its hole.

"I once saw a striped squirrel on a rail fence with some kind of weed in his mouth—it could have been a milkweed seed. At any length, he scudded swiftly along the middle rail past me, and instead of running over or around the posts, he glided through the little hole in the post left above the rails as swiftly as if there had been no post in the way. So he sped through five posts in succession in a straight line! But you say they are not social creatures?

"Why, I can remember one October afternoon in 1857 when I saw as many as twenty striped squirrels busily running out to the ends of the twigs, biting off the nuts, running back and taking off the acorn cups, and storing the nuts away in their cheeks."

"I doubt if they were working together," I told him. "Although they have learned to live in man's vicinity, they are fiercely independent. I've often thought they would be a better symbol for America than the eagle. After all, except for the sheer joy of running about, they continually work. The great naturalist John Burroughs once described a Catskill chipmunk that carried home five quarts of hickory nuts and one quart of chestnuts during a three-day period."

"But why independent?" he asked.

"Except during mating season early in the spring or in July, chipmunks live alone. The female takes care of two litters a year, usually consisting of between three and five youngsters, born in an underground chamber. But most of the time, chipmunks are loners."

"I know I've heard the chattering of chipmunks on many occasions," he said. "One time in 1853, I heard a striped squirrel in the wall near me, as if he blew a short blast on a dry leaf."

"It's amazing to watch a mother chipmunk raise her young," I said. "They continually chatter, but if she lowers her voice just a bit, the youngsters will stop their play and run like the scamps they are into their family hole. Later, juvenile chippers move into unoccupied burrows, and if they can't find an old home, they will build anew."

## The White-tailed Deer

"What do you think about the deer?" I asked.

"Well, they are regular creatures. I notice that cows never walk abreast, but in single file commonly, making a narrow cow-path, or the herd walks in a loose wedge. They retain still the habit of all the deer tribe—acquired when the earth was all covered with forest—of traveling from necessity in narrow paths in the woods."

He stopped to pour another cup of tea.

"The deer that run in the woods, as the moose for instance, carry perfect trees on their heads. The French call them *bois*. No wonder there are fables of centaurs and the like. No wonder there is a story of a hunter who, when his bullets failed, fired cherry-stones into the heads of his game and so trees sprouted out of them, and the hunter refreshed himself with the cherries. It's a perfect piece of mythology which belongs to these days."

"I looked up the scientific name last night," I told him. "It's *Odocoileus virginianus*, the genus referring to the tooth structure, and the species to Virginia, where they were apparently first spotted."

"Back in January of 1855," said Thoreau, "I was reading William Wood's *New England's Prospect*. There were then complaints of the wolf as the great devourer of bear, moose, and deer. Of the deer, there were a great many, even more in the Massachusetts Bay, more than in any other place. It was reported that some hunters killed sixteen deer in one day on Deer Island in Boston Harbor, where they had swum to avoid the wolves."

"Well, never fear," I said. "Over the years, thanks to an early twentieth-century revulsion to predators and the decline of American farms leaving many abandoned fields and pastures, and despite the fact that hunting is now a major industry in many states, deer are on the increase. And gardens are continually threatened."

"What would you recommend?"

"I'd like to see the predators return, and if that fails, controlled thinning of the herds, as they do in England."

"I read a book back in 1861," mused Thoreau, "called *Carolina Sports by Land and Water*, by one Hon. William Elliott. He described pursuing a deer, which he had wounded. He tried to run him down with his horse, but, as he tells us, 'The noble animal refused to trample on his fellow quadruped,' so he made up for it by kicking the deer in the side of the head with his spurred boot. The deer entered a thicket and Elliott was compelled to pursue the panting animal on foot.

A large fallen oak lies across his path; he gathers himself up for the leap, and falls exhausted directly across it. Before he could recover his legs, and while he lay thus poised on the tree, I fling myself at full length upon the body of the struggling deer—my left hand clasps his neck, while my right detaches the knife; whose fatal blade, in another moment, is buried in his throat. There he lay in his blood, and I remained sole occupant of the field.

"There's a picture on the opposite page which shows the hunter in the act of stabbing the deer."

"So much for heroics," I said.

## Cats in the Garden

"How do you feel about cats in the garden?" I asked Thoreau.

"I can remember one time back in 1850 when I was working on my journal and somebody in the house shut the cat's tail in the door. She made such a caterwaul as had driven two whole words out of my thoughts. I saw unspeakable things in the sky and looming in the horizon of my mind, and now they were all reduced to a cat's tail. Vast films of thought floated through my brain, like clouds pregnant with rain enough to fertilize and restore a world, and suddenly they were all dissipated."

"That reminds me of a poem from childhood," I told him:

There is music in the hammer,
There is music in the nail,
There is music in the kitty,
When you step upon its tail."

"I've often wondered how, so often, a man is more humanely related to a cat or dog than to any human being. What bond is it relates us to any animal we keep in the house but the bond of affection? In a degree, we grow to love one another."

"They've done studies in recent years that show having a pet like a cat or a dog extends the life of the owner, but so far they cannot explain how. But I know that having a good hunting cat in the garden takes care of a number of problems—they keep the rabbit population down and hunt and dispatch voles."

"What are voles?"

"Voles are tailless mice. You know, Danny Meadow Mouse in the *Burgess Bedtime Stories* by Gelett Burgess. Oh, that's right; he was born four years after you died, so you never heard about the purple cow poem or the anthropomorphizing of voles.

"They are little brown furry animals under five inches long with a prodigious appetite both for food and reproduction. Each vole can eat its own weight in twenty-four hours, and a population of fifteen to an acre can increase to 250 in four years. When people talk about mole damage, they usually are describing garden horrors perpetrated by voles, not moles."

"What havoc do they sow?"

"They burrow through hay mulches and tunnel through leaf piles, and eat, eat, then eat some more. Wherever possible they gnaw on tree bark, chew around bushes, and they've even ripped up the leaves of lamb's-tongue in the herb garden for nest linings."

"Moles I know," he said. "Back in June of 1856, I remember watching a star-nosed mole endeavoring in vain to bury himself in the sand and gravel while men were repairing a large hole at the railroad turntable. Some inhuman fellow had cut off its tail. It was blue-black with much fur, a very thick, plump animal, apparently some four inches long, but he shortened himself a third or more. His forefeet were large and set sidewise on their edges, and he used these to shovel dirt aside, while his large, long, and starred snout was feeling the way and breaking ground. I carried him along to plowed ground, where he buried himself in a minute or two."

"Moles are meat-eaters, not plant-eaters. They live almost entirely underground, feeding on smaller animal life, especially earthworms and grubs. They are not vegetarians, only chewing enough roots to clear a path through an underground jungle."

The sun was getting higher, and despite the shade of countless leaves, it was getting warmer. Thoreau adjusted himself on his chair, and picking his hat up off the ground, gave it a pat or two before putting it on his head.

"So the cats eat the voles," he said.

"Yes. Our garden cat, Miss Jekyll, has always done her bit with the vole menace: Every afternoon, a freshly killed subject shows up on the doormat. And I am sure she has dispatched many more out in the garden and the fields beyond.

"For all the talk about cats killing birds," I said, "I would never want a garden without a resident cat. And, I suppose, I could always put a bell on any animal that begins to make too much of a dent in the birdlife."

"One morning in October of 1858," Thoreau concluded, "the garden was alive with migrating sparrows and the cat came in from an early walk amid the weeds. She was full of sparrows and wanted no breakfast that morning, unless it was a saucer of milk, the dear creature. I saw her studying ornithology between the cornrows."

## An Interview with Dr. Leonard Lee Rue III

A year is a long time. If it's spring in your backyard and some violets, or perhaps trilliums, are blooming, when you think back to the last time you saw those blooms and you remember all the passing days and the events they saw, a year is a long time. It's also a long time from a deer's point of view.

So I called Dr. Leonard Lee Rue III to ask him about a year in the life of a deer.

Dr. Rue is an imposing man: piercing eyes, a craggy face surrounded with a salt and pepper beard and mustache, plus a head full of long, gray hair. He's the author of twenty-eight books on wildlife, and his photographs have appeared in countless magazines, from *Field & Stream* to *Newsweek*. He lives in Blairstown, New Jersey. And he doesn't accept e-mail—which is a laudable trait.

## The Spring

"In the spring," he said, "snows melt and days get longer. It's a clue to the whitetails of the North to move. Many deer have been yarding up, a term that means they've wintered in a sheltered area, like a gully, a swamp, or just a protected place in the woods, to get out of the wind. These are warmer spots where the sun by day and the tree canopy by night make and hold a bit of heat. In the West, mule deer and blacktails move to lowlands, rather than yarding up.

"The driving force is food. In spring more than any other time of the year, sprouting vegetation provides nutrition. Believe it or not, throughout all of North America, wherever it's grown (over thirty million acres in the U.S.), in early spring deer feed on alfalfa."

"Are there distinct behavior patterns for males and females at this time of the year?" I asked.

"All over the country, bucks bed down earlier in the morning and look for heavier cover. They're generally less active by day and only come out to feed later in the evening. And don't forget, in the springtime whitetail bucks are often solitary or sometimes a big buck is followed about by several younger bucks. Blacktails are usually the same. Remember, their antlers are growing now and they take special care not to injure themselves.

"Does, on the other hand, usually start feeding around dawn and continue until about 9:00 A.M. Pregnant females have additional demands on their systems and they need a long time to cram in all the food necessary. Then they rest until around 11:00 A.M."

"I remember," I said, "that up on our Sullivan County farm, their activities often had clockwork precision."

"That's right," agreed Dr. Rue, "and they start to feed again around 4:00 P.M., the time when they eat the most. Once they have their fawns, the does usually nurse them before each of their own feeding periods begin.

"As birthing time approaches, a doe seeks solitude. When a fawn is born, it's out of proportion to an adult: The legs are much longer at birth than later in life; in fact, they seem to be all legs. And a doe can give birth to identical twins, fraternal twins, triplets, or even quadruplets—although fraternal twins are more common than identical twins."

"Humans have something psychologists call the 'cuteness response'," I said. "It's why even the most masculine of men will *ooh* and *ah* over a baby, or any young animal— or even an adult with no adult features, no sharp edges, but who has big, round eyes. And if ever there was such an animal, it's a fawn. I can just imagine people's responses to twins."

"Every year," he continued, "game departments across the country are deluged with reports of folks picking up 'orphan' fawns. They are obviously both being protective and caught in the spell of the fawn's beauty. Unless the doe has been killed, these fawns are not orphans, but once touched and petted, there's a 10-percent chance that they may become orphans. If the mother is afraid of a human scent, she might abandon her fawn.

"After a doe washes her newborn fawn, she leads it away from the birthing spot. That wash not only cleans the fawn but also leaves a doe's individual odor so she can tell her offspring from others.

"Now she must nurse the fawn. Fawns spend about 96 percent of their time curled up in their beds. When bedded, they hold their heads up and are very, very alert."

"I know the spotted coat makes excellent camouflage," I said, "because I remember that one spring, as Jean and I were walking in the woods and passed an area of beautiful ferns dappled with sunlight, we suddenly saw a fawn. It didn't move a muscle, but we looked into those sorrowful eyes and quickly, quietly walked on."

"I've often seen dogs run unaware right past fawns that were curled up in the forest," Dr. Rue noted. "Many biologists claim that a young fawn has no discernable odor."

## The Summer

Soon it's summer in the forest. When walking in the Catskill woods, even in the shade of old oaks, you could smell the scent of pitch from the pines.

"It's the only time of the year," said Dr. Rue, "that deer, including the doe with her young, can take it slow and easy.

"From birth, fawns are on a milk diet. But starting at about three weeks, they follow their mothers and begin to sample all sorts of vegetation. By the age of five weeks, they've become quite selective in what they eat and have actually begun to develop taste preferences. Research has shown that fawns are dependent on milk until they are about three months old, but I think the speed of weaning depends on the individual doe.

"And let's not forget play! Play is conditioning for later life and most mammals engage in it. Even a solitary fawn will suddenly run, buck, kick out, jump, and dash around in circles. If there's more than one, they'll play tag, all the while developing their muscles, expanding lung capacity, and learning the dexterity needed to escape from predators later in life.

"By the end of August, the fawns begin to lose their spots and all deer start to shed their thin, red summer coats, taking on their hollow-haired, grayish-brown winter coats."

Dr. Rue stopped for moment. "Ever been bitten by a deer fly?" he asked.

"Certainly," I answered. "And up in the Catskills they get pretty big, too."

"Well," he said, "deer are subject to all the discomforts of a camper in the wood, in addition to many internal parasites. Deerflies, midges, blackflies, and mosquitoes do their worst, not to mention ticks which can carry Lyme disease.

"And they are subject to an army of different worms, flukes, and other diseases including anthrax. They even get tumors."

"When you really think about it," I said, "it's a wonder so many survive. They fight nature, man, disease, predators, famine, cold, automobiles, and loss of range. But they still go on."

"Yes, it is. And in the summer nature picks up the slack. While does and fawns come out just before sunset, the bucks feed at dusk. The deer begin to feed around 11:00 P.M. and again after 1:00 A.M., with another major feeding effort just before dawn. By midsummer, the buck's antlers have reached their maximum growth, with daylight stimulating the pituitary gland, which in turn causes the testicles to enlarge and produce sperm. The antlers harden and their velvet covering dries up. The velvet is stripped from the antlers, always starting at the tips. A buck picks a bendable sapling—not a tree—and rubs his antlers along the trunk.

"Now, with hardened antlers and testosterone in his blood, the buck reaches the peak of its masculinity."

## The Autumn

In autumn the days are shorter, and in the mountains cool air flows down the valleys. At higher elevations, leaves are touched by frost, while on clear, moonless nights, the stars glow as though lit by special lighting," began Dr. Rue.

"Deer are greatly influenced by weather and the phases of the moon," he continued. "They know that winter is on the way, so they begin to eat compulsively, taking advantage of the available food. I can state unequivocally that in the northeastern, central, southern, and west coast regions of the United States, acorns, when available, are the favorite food of white-tailed deer. Acorns are very important to both the mule deer and blacktails, as well.

"And, just as people get indigestion, deer can suffer from overeating, especially from too much high-carbohydrate food, like corn, sugar beets, grapes, pears, or wheat. When autumn winds cause a surplus of apples to fall, the deer eat too many and get indigestion."

"We had a number of apple trees on our property," I said. "And when the apples lay upon the ground too long, they began to ferment—with the result that an occasional grouse would get blotto. On two afternoons, we had deer stumble and flounce about just like people who have had too many drinks."

"I've never seen it myself," he said, "but I've read many reports of such behavior.

"About this time, the fawns are two-thirds the size of their mothers, and are perfect little carbon copies. They actually stop growing now and wait until the spring, because all the nutrition they take in is necessary for winter survival.

"And now rutting begins. Sexual activity peaks in November and December, although timing depends on the latitude. It's a dangerous time, and about three weeks before the first females come into estrus, the bucks start to run the does. When this country was primarily rural, it was said that the most dangerous animal was a Jersey bull. With the passing of the farms, the most dangerous animal is now a pet whitetail buck. Every year there are stories of people being killed or injured by a buck they raised in captivity.

"Then hunting season begins, with some states only permitting the shooting of bucks. But whatever the rules, the game is afoot."

"When we lived in the Catskills, we dreaded hunting season," I said. "Not because of the genuine hunters, but because of what we called 'slob hunters.' They came up to the mountains to prove their manhood, using a lot of beer and noise for cover, and every year shot as many of each other as they did the deer."

"I know," he said. "I know the slob is the one who blazes away at anything, at any time, and at any distance. Decent hunters will never try for a 'pot' or 'luck' shot, but always make sure their weapons kill the game cleanly and quickly if they shoot.

"When you realize how many wounded deer are lost every year, the figures become appalling—ranging all the way to 80 percent of the total hunter's take."

## The Winter

Soon the chill winds blow, cold rains pelt the earth, and the snows begin to fall.

"Some deer will yard up, while others roam a small area of woods, and food becomes scarce," said Dr. Rue. "It's now that farms, nurseries, and gardens are hit harder. The deer are forced to do more browsing in the winter, although browsing can serve as a sort of pruning and most plants survive.

"But when the easily reached food is gone, deer can stand on their hind legs and reach overhead branches. A seven-month-old fawn standing on its hind legs can reach up about five feet, an adult doe can get up to six feet, and a buck up to seven."

"And people must remember," I said, "that these behavior patterns were set long before farms and gardens dotted the countryside. Under nature's eyes, a shorn tree that lives is still a tree—not a blot on the aesthetic landscape of a gardener."

"And with so many deer," he said, "and habitats decreasing, the saddest thing of all is the starvation that haunts so many of these animals. Sure, some fawns have been known to go a month without food and still survive; some adults have gone up to two months. But more than that and starvation sets in.

"Add to that winter recreation, with snowmobiles forcing frightened deer to use scant reserves of energy just to escape what they perceive as a major threat.

"The Indians called the month of February, 'Starvation Moon'; it was thought to be the month of greatest winter hardship. The effects of a severe winter are insidious. The obvious loss is indicated by the carcasses of starved deer found in the spring, their bleaching bones scattered about. But less obvious is the drop in birthrate the following spring."

Dr. Rue paused for a moment and his mouth produced a slight smile.

"But deer," he said, "have a tremendous tenacity; they are tough. Although many will die, more will live, and it has always been so. They've lived with adversity for many millions of years and have evolved because of it."

## An Interview with Benjamin Wechsler

Benjamin Wechsler is an old Sullivan County resident, a friend and colleague for thirty-three years. Over those years I've served on many Sullivan County committees with Mr. Wechsler, including one group formed by New York State to preserve the future Neversink Gorge State Park, an effort doomed to failure because the state felt it had the moral authority to abrogate hunting and fishing rights.

I've been one of those lucky people who have roamed this gorge in good weather and in bad, and have enjoyed walking through age-worn rock that in places looks like Angkor Wat and in others, the forest primeval.

The gorge is located a few miles outside of Monticello, the biggest city in Sullivan County. It's within a two-hour drive of New York City, and since the middle of the 1900s has been a focal point for tourism and hunting.

Mr. Wechsler knows a lot about deer. He's been running various hunting clubs since the Second World War. And he's one of those observers of nature who tries to figure out just what a hungry deer will do, so he can think ahead and outsmart the devils before they invade his garden.

"Deer," he said, "are a cursed species: They eat up to fourteen hours a day, nibbling here, grazing there, then after that's finished they have to chew a cud. They're grazing animals with little time to think but a lot of time spent in survival. Unlike predators, they have no time to really think, no time to develop beyond a certain point, no time to sit around and digest the food and happenings of the day—just time to eat, and in many cases that's being denied to them."

I asked him about the history of deer in that part of New York State as it relates to conditions in the rest of the country.

"There was staggering overpopulation in the 1960s," he said, "so it's difficult to believe that, until the early 1900s, there were no laws—deer were shot for food and for hurting crops. The population fell to drastic levels, so to restock the Catskills they brought deer in from the Adirondacks.

"Then subsistence farms were abandoned and dairy farms went into decline. Open fields soon gave way to second growth, beginning with poplars, birch, sumac, and other fast-growing trees. Then the older-living species arrived, like oaks, maples, beech, and white pines, so the deer now had new food sources.

"History entered into the equation, and by the end of World War II, nine out of ten hunters were away fighting in the armed services.

"By the late 1960s, the deer were once again eating themselves out of house and home. You would actually find dead deer while walking through the woods. They began to eat bark, damaged trees, and went into the orchards. Finally the climate began to change, resulting in less mast, and except for feral dogs, there were no predators to keep the animals in check.

"Now the predators are back and bears are also becoming a nuisance. Coyotes, too. Thirty years ago you saw feral cats and feral dogs, but in the last five years the deer have been attacked by coyotes. In the woods, coyote scat is replacing deer scat. Luckily, coyotes practice a territorial birth control based on packs competing in territories. At some point they produce fewer puppies per year per pack. So hopefully down the line there will be a new balance between coyotes and whitetails."

"Deer," said Ben, "are suspicious creatures. I remember one summer, after a wild thunder and lightning storm, a huge branch fell from one of my apple trees and landed in the tall grass next to the trunk. There was no fencing, so the local deer herd was free to move about. The first day they just circled and looked at the fallen branch. The second day they ate about a third of the leaves, the next day they finished another third, and finally, on the fourth day, except for the large branches, they finished it off.

"I know that some people curse the deer for destroying precious plants. I know that if you live in the suburbs or as I do, in the country, you've got to do more than curse if you want to protect your plants."

I can remember visiting Ben in the spring. Whenever he decided to put in a special tree or an interesting plant, he surrounded the specimen with chicken wire.

"Dogs," said Ben, "are great! Deer do not like dogs, and sometimes I wonder if deer have a collective memory of past experiences out-running and out-leaping large, barking dogs.

"But in the end," he concluded, "you must fence. It's really the only safe way of protecting your plants and your property."

## *A Visit with The Wild Gardener*

### Our Friends, the Deer: "Klaatu Barada Nicto!"

Yesterday I felt like one of the unlucky characters in a Stephen King novel—not the one about the rabid dog or the giant rats under the New England cotton mill, more like the man imprisoned by the rabid fan. Only, instead of being human, my fans are those goats of the woods, those so-called "Bambis," who (often with reason) prune every garden they can find.

With horror I looked out into the garden: Three of them were happily munching on the hyacinth and had chewed back all the Allegheny spurge, leaving stumps.

I rapped on the window with such force that my knuckles turned white. I yelled. They turned, batted their perfectly curled eyelashes in my direction, and went back to munching.

Running out the back door, I screamed: "Out! Out! Out!"

With a flick of their tails, they strutted away.

Not only had they eaten the spurge and the bulbs, they had nibbled the emerging hostas, clipped the daylilies, and chewed off many of the buds on the flowering crab apple.

I remember when we first moved to the country, I had always thought of deer in terms of that fine melodrama, *All That Heaven Allows,* in which Rock Hudson plays a younger man who romances an older widow, Jane Wyman.

In the final scene, they share an embrace in the old mill and look out on the garden as a young doe, oozing cuteness, prances up to the window and gently takes a ripened apple from the snow-swept ground.

Oh, heart! Oh, rapture!

Today I view deer as intelligent goats ready to act as tanks with hooves and mow down anything green except burdocks, crabgrass, and goutweed. Their rule is: If it's valuable or attractive, tear it to shreds!

Conservationists advise you to put up a fence. Well, those of you who have tried know that it has to be over ten feet high—and that's when there isn't any snow on the ground. For every foot of packed snow, add a foot to your fence. And be sure every inch is staked to the ground, as the little loves can easily crawl under. To fence any reasonably sized garden, it would take enough money to finance a trip to Paris for two months.

I thought it might be time to report on a few items of deer research published in *Pacific Horticulture*.

"Gardeners," they report, "have experimented with many defenses against deer. Dr. Kenneth Stocking, who heads the arboretum at Sonoma State College, says that an emulsion of blood meal sprinkled on favored plants after each rain or burst of growth helps to repel deer.*

Note that phrase: "after each rain." It means that only in areas of minimum rainfall would such treatment be practical; in most places one would need the cooperation of Dracula to get enough blood to do a good job.

Big-game repellents sprayed on foliage are reported by some to be effective, but these must be replenished as new growth emerges. A neighbor tried dipping strips of cloth in Deer-Away repeatedly for two weeks. Tied to green garden stakes about four feet high and planted throughout her rose bed, these strips kept deer away for two months before the whole affair had to be repeated. On a larger scale . . . the repellent, however, wore off in the first few rains and repeated use was not cost effective.

Roy Davidson, a gardener in Seattle, reports that a Bellevue, Washington, firm called INKO has developed a slow-release selenium compound in pellet form that can be applied in big aspirin-like tablets to the soil, where it dissolves slowly and is absorbed by the roots of trees. It is said to be effective in protecting fruit trees, which give off a garlic odor.

The best advice I found in the article is to lay six-foot-wide strips of chicken wire on cleared ground around the garden because deer do not like to get their hooves caught in the openings. Or try the New Zealand deer fence, which, laid at an angle, appears three feet wide to an approaching deer.

In years past we always fed the deer corn. This kept them out of the garden during the winter, leaving all our shrubs and dwarf conifers free from nibbling. Then, as the fields greened up, they went off and left the plants alone.

The year before last we fed seventeen deer every day, once in the morning and once at night. Contrary to the claims of many conservation offices, this does not destroy their independence; the minute the grass greens up, they leave the corn, retune their stomachs, and go off to pillage all the farms in the neighborhood.

We didn't feed them this year because the herd never showed. For a moment I began to believe the cries of many local hunters that the herd had been destroyed. I patted myself on the shoulder and decided to rest. After years of angst, I was finally free. Bambi was gone. Hallelujah!

No such luck.

On winter walks I began to see deer tracks where I had not seen them before. Then, by the end of February, the dog and I started seeing them in the woods. At first there were shadowy outlines, like Kirk and Spock just before "beaming up"; I thought it was my imagination at work. Just past Valentine's Day, the outlines grew more vivid and I realized that the deer were still there, merely walking different paths.

In a field down the road from us, I saw great numbers of them, sharing turf with the turkeys, and the count continued to go up.

Four entered our back field towards the end of March, and I chalked it up to mere caprice. More fool I.

I now wish for Gort. Remember Gort? He was the magnificent robot in *The Day the Earth Stood Still.* A usually peaceful killing machine that could, with the proper code word, wreak havoc beyond description and that had the power to annihilate the Earth.

If Gort were here, I would point to the deer. And unlike Patricia Neal, I would not say: "*Klaatu barada nicto!*"

# The Triple Threat

# 3

For all their innocence, deer can cause many problems for people: They are vectors for a number of diseases that affect humans, notably Lyme disease; they are factors in thousands of traffic accidents each year; and they cause vast amounts of damage not only to home gardens but to commercial nurseries and tree farms—and yes, in isolated communities, every garden is at risk.

## The Threat of Lyme Disease

At the end of the 1970s, the residents of Sullivan County, New York, first heard local hunters talking about a dread new disease that attacked people, revolved about deer, and was transmitted by ticks. The infection was called Lyme disease, so named because it was first observed in Lyme, Connecticut, where in 1975 a group of local children came down with arthritic symptoms that baffled doctors. Further investigation led to the discovery that Lyme disease was caused by a bacterium, a member of the group known as spirochetes, the same group responsible for syphilis.

Late in the nineteenth century, European doctors had described the disease, and experts believe it's been over here for about a hundred years. Earlier in the twentieth century, European doctors examined patients who evidenced a reddish rash that was associated with tick bites, called *erythema migrans* or EM. Theory suggested it was caused by a tick-borne bacterium. By the 1940s, more tick-borne diseases were observed that began with EM and developed into other illnesses. By the end of that decade, spirochetes had been found in skin samples and the new wonder drug, penicillin, was prescribed as a treatment. In 1969 a doctor in Wisconsin diagnosed a patient with EM and prescribed penicillin for a successful treatment.

But in 1975 those thirty children and adults in Lyme developed what looked like cases of rheumatoid arthritis. Because some of the children lived on the same street, the Connecticut State Department of Health was called in to investigate.

The infections around Lyme led researchers to believe that the presence of EM and the arthritis symptoms were linked to tick bites, and that penicillin treatment not only diminished the EM but also reduced the risk of subsequent arthritic symptoms.

In 1982 Dr. Willy Burgdorf, a scientist from the National Institutes of Health, discovered spirochetes in the mid-gut of the adult deer tick (*Ixodes scapularis*). The bacteria were christened *Borrelia burgdorfei* or Bb for short. Since then antibiotics have been the general treatment for the disease.

Lyme disease has been reported in every continental state except Montana, and New York has the highest rate of occurrence in the country (hence the concern in Sullivan County). Between 1980 and July of 2002, there were 179,279 reported cases of Lyme disease.

In the Northeast and the north-central United States, the tick-carrier of choice is the blacklegged tick (*I. scapularis*); on the Pacific Coast, the western blacklegged tick (*I. pacificus*) does the job.

There are over 850 species of tick in the U.S., all belonging to one of five genera: *Amblyomma*, the lone-star tick; *Dermacentor*, the American dog tick; *Ixodes*, the blacklegged and Western blacklegged ticks); and *Ornithodoros* and *Rhipicephalus*, the brown dog ticks.

Deer ticks are tiny, much smaller and harder to find than adult dog ticks. In their juvenile stages they're about the size of a pinhead. Unless engorged with blood, even when attacking they are so small that people easily miss them. The largest deer tick is less than three-sixteenths of an inch, legs extended. And to make matters worse, multiple diseases can be contracted from a single tick bite.

Most people believe ticks to be insects; they are not. Insects have six legs and three body segments, while adult ticks have eight legs and two body segments. Ticks are arachnids, close relatives of spiders, mites, and chiggers. Ticks are bloodsucking parasites that feed on people, wild

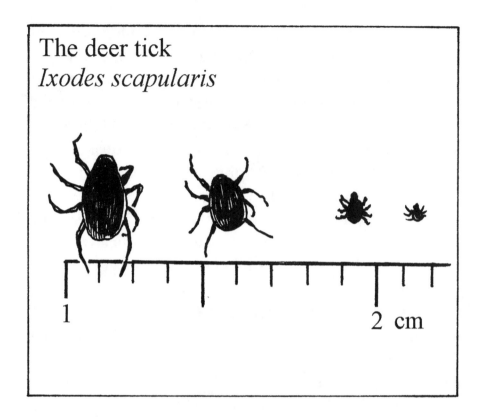

The deer tick
*Ixodes scapularis*

1                                    2 cm

and domestic mammals, birds, reptiles, and even other arachnids.

A mature tick usually climbs a tall blade of grass, the fronds of a fern, or leaves of a weed, at a spot slightly above ground level. Then it looks for a host using a number of incredibly complex methods, including monitoring its victim's carbon dioxide levels, body heat, or other chemical alerts. When all systems are go, it uses its forelegs to grab the skin, clothing, or fur of a host.

The female tick requires a blood meal in order to lay eggs, so finding a host is a survival strategy. Clutching their victim's skin, ticks draw blood using specialized mouthparts adorned with harpoon-like barbs in reverse, designed to penetrate first, then attach to skin. They also secrete a cement-like substance that helps them hold fast to their host. They are totally dependent on the blood and tissue fluids of the host. The longer an infective tick feeds, the greater the chance of infection, with infection almost guaranteed if ticks feed in one spot for two or more days.

Ticks go through four life states: egg, larva, nymph, and adult. Eggs hatch into larva, a tiny being with six legs. It feeds and molts or changes into an eight-legged nymph. The nymph feeds and molts into an adult. To infect a victim with a disease, the tick must keep its infection through all stages of development. Some ticks can and some ticks cannot. Luckily, even though dog ticks can pick up Lyme disease, they do not carry the bacteria from one molt to another.

Who gets a tick? People who work or live in and around tick-infested woods and fields are at risk of contracting Lyme disease. Even suburbanites with clean and manicured backyards, who use the outdoors for recreation, are at risk.

## Getting Rid of a Tick

I went to the Web site of the Lyme Disease Foundation (www.lyme.org) for the following up-to-date information on removing a tick:

1. Using a fine-point tweezers, grasp the tick at the place of attachment, as close to the skin as possible. Gently pull the tick straight out.
2. Place the tick in a small vial labeled with the victim's name and address, and the date.
3. Wash your hands and disinfect the tweezers and bite site.
4. Mark your calendar with the victim's name, place of tick attachment on the body, and general health at the time.
5. Call your doctor to determine if treatment is warranted.
6. Monitor the tick-bite site and the victim's general health for signs or symptoms of a tick-borne illness. Make sure you mark any changes in health status on your calendar. If possible, have the tick tested by a lab, your local health department, or a veterinarian.

Having on many occasions botched the job of removing dog ticks (not to mention common slivers), the following frequently asked question at their Web site seemed more than pertinent: If the mouthparts break off in the skin, should I dig them out?

The Foundation has heard two competing opinions about this. One states that the mouthparts can cause a secondary infection and should be removed like a splinter. The other states that parents can do more harm by trying to hold down a child and digging out the mouthparts with a needle. One pediatrician advises to leave the mouthparts, and as skin sloughs off, the tick parts will come out on their own.

You should also observe the following cautions:

1. Children should be taught to seek adult help for tick removal.
2. If you must remove a tick with your fingers, use a tissue or leaf to avoid contact with infected tick fluids.
3. Do not prick, crush, or burn the tick because it may release infected fluids or tissue.
4. Do not try to smother the tick with household preparations like petroleum jelly or nail polish— the attached tick has enough oxygen on its own to complete the feeding.

## Why Is Lyme Disease Spreading?

It's not only deer. Studies have shown that migratory birds have helped disperse infected ticks. Dogs and other animals can run in infected fields and bring infected ticks back to suburban yards. Dogs traveling with their owners can spread infected ticks to distant locations. After all, people think nothing of traveling thousands of miles with their pets.

## Lyme Disease in Dogs

Just when you thought it was safe to come out of the house, there's another problem on the horizon: Lyme disease in dogs.

Lyme disease problems have increased 16-fold since 1982. It has been reported in 47 states, and is being reported with increasing frequency each year. What's more, the incidence in dogs may be six to ten times higher.

Ask yourself these questions:

- Do you take your dog on walks?
- Does your dog travel with you?
- Do you take your dog camping?
- Does your dog "tag along"?
- Does your dog hunt with you?
- Does your dog come along on family picnics?
- Do you take your dog jogging?
- Does your dog go to parks?

Answering yes to any of the above means that your dog is potentially in contact with ticks.

Lyme disease was first reported in dogs in 1984. Since then, it has spread rapidly across the country, affecting a greater number of victims every year.

We called on an old friend and retired Sullivan County veterinarian, Dr. George Hahn, for the latest on dogs, ticks, and disease.

He was decidedly upbeat about the threat.

Only about 5 to 10 percent of all dogs tested have tested positive for Lyme disease. Of those 5 to 10 percent, about 5 to 10 percent do not show any symptoms, which may indicate there may be more who have it but don't show it. The answer, of course, is for pet owners to take care of their dogs.

And don't forget to check your cats, too.

## How is Lyme Disease Treated in Dogs?

Several broad-spectrum antibiotics have proven effective in treating Lyme disease, especially in its early stages. Your veterinarian will have the most effective remedy available.

Just to be on the safe side, brush your dog after each outing. In fact, routinely check your pets after they have been outdoors, especially if they have been in areas with tall grass and brush. Cut brush and mow the grass where your pet plays. Ask your veterinarian about vaccinating your pet.

## Controlling Ticks on Your Person

Whether you still venture out of doors or decide to sit out all the threats by staying inside until winter, ticks don't take a holiday until they freeze. But there are a number of simple things you can do to avoid ticks.

The best protection is prevention. Do not go out in the woods in late spring, summer, or early fall dressed in short-shorts and flip-flop sandals. You will get exactly what you deserve.

If you do wear shorts, be sure they are walking shorts and your feet and lower legs are encased in good socks. If you plan to walk off a path, trade in the shorts for long pants and wear a long-sleeved shirt.

Next is textile choice. It's necessary to choose light-colored clothing (like khaki) so you or somebody walking close by can see an insect or a tick climbing up your back, aiming for the neck. In fact, it's a good idea to stop for a tick check at least every half hour.

For a miticide, tickicide, or insecticide, try DEET—not pleasant, but it generally works. Liberally apply this lotion around your ankles, wrists, and waistline, underneath and on top of clothing, and use more if you are prone to sweating.

Any tick that gets past your defenses must be removed. If you have no tweezers or forceps in your first aid pack, use your fingers—but after tick removal, carefully wash your hands. If a tick has been imbedded for more than a few hours, see a doctor.

Finally, upon returning home, check again for ticks. And don't forget to comb the dog, because dogs are walking tick magnets.


## Wasting Disease

Believe it or not, there's another tick threat on the horizon and it's called wasting disease.

Chronic Wasting Disease, or CWD, attacks the central nervous system of white-tailed deer, mule deer, and Rocky Mountain elk, causing fatal damage to the brain. It is spread by a newly discovered disease vector called a prion. Prions are mutated proteins that cause normal proteins to fold in abnormal ways, resulting in sponge-like holes in the brain. The disease is similar to, but significantly different from, scrapie, a disease found in sheep and first documented more than 400 years ago.

In the later stages of infection, deer and elk with CWD exhibit progressive weight loss, listlessness, excessive salivation and urination, increased water intake, depression, and, eventually, death. Animals can be infected with CWD for months or years before outward signs appear.

While the exact method of transmission of CWD is not known, most scientists believe it travels from animal to animal through body fluids like feces, urine, or saliva. Animals that are crowded or confined have a greater chance of encountering the body fluids of other animals and therefore a higher likelihood of becoming infected. It's also a problem with animals that have social customs that include close contact with herdmates. There is a high probability that CWD prions survive in the environment after infected and exposed animals are removed.

At present, CWD is unique to North America. It has been found in wild deer and elk in Colorado, Wyoming, Nebraska, South Dakota, Wisconsin, and Saskatchewan. It has been found in captive animals in Colorado, Montana, South Dakota, Oklahoma, Kansas, Nebraska, Saskatchewan, and Alberta.

Currently, the only test for the disease is a microscopic examination of an animal's brain stem—to do this, the animal must be destroyed.

There is, at present, no scientific evidence that CWD can infect humans, either through direct contact or by eating the meat of infected animals. But while the chance of transmission is extremely small or nonexistent, it's always best not to harvest any animal that appears sick or is acting strange. Note the animal's location and contact the local game commission. Avoid cutting or puncturing the spinal cords or brains of animals taken in areas where CWD occurs. Do not use household utensils to field dress or process your deer. Wear rubber or latex gloves when handling any harvested animal.

## On the Road

Jean and I have experienced traffic accidents involving deer, twice!

The first was back in the late 1970s while driving back on a country road from Monticello, New York, late on a spring night. The radio was tuned to WQXR out of Manhattan, the air smelled of new foliage and a recent rain, and a slim moon was breaking through the clouds. I was driving about thirty-five miles per hour and we were talking about a new book I was going to begin the following week.

Up ahead on the left was a local tavern, its parking lot pretty full. And on the right was a yellow warning sign, with the silhouette of an upright deer, clearly visible in my headlights.

Suddenly, from in front of the sign, a stag leapt out of the woods, stopped for a moment as my headlights dazzled his eyes, then proceeded to jump across the road at the same time my right front fender hit him broadside.

I hit the brakes as hard as I could.

The entire front end of the car (a fairly new Plymouth) was smashed, the windshield broke into large shards, the tire went flat, and the poor creature struggled on the blood-stained pavement.

I pulled Jean out of the front seat on the driver's side and we ran to the tavern ahead. An alert barkeeper already knew something was wrong—he had heard the crash.

"We just hit a deer," I said, my voice shaking with emotion.

"I heard it," he said, and reaching above his head, grabbed a rifle that hung on the wall between two bent deer hoofs.

He went out the door and seconds later we heard a shot.

The other folks in the bar came up to find out if we were OK, and the bartender's wife poured us each a shot of whisky. Though usually wine drinkers, we drank it down.

It was only a half hour to closing so Frank, the bartender and owner, helped us push the car into his lot and later drove us the ten miles home. The next morning we called our local garage for a tow and a major repair job.

The experience was never forgotten, and even today, some thirty years later, I can still smell the night and the blood on the road.

Our next experience was driving up Route 97 from Port Jervis, a picturesque road that winds and curves along the Delaware River to the small town of Hancock. This time it was raining, but as we left Port Jervis and began climbing the hills to Narrowsburg, the rain began to turn to ice. At one particular hill near Grassy Swamp Road, I could feel the wheels slipping.

With an effort, I kept the car running along at about thirty miles an hour, knowing that if I slowed we would slip and be stuck there for the night.

Suddenly Jean shouted: "Look out your window. My God, there's a deer running beside us!"

With my right hand on the wheel, I opened the driver's window to confront a terrified eye and flared nostrils—steam and all—and heard the sound of hooves slipping on the iced macadam in both fast and slow motion.

Before the doe could slip or directly turn into the side of the car, I pressed my foot on the accelerator and pushed-slid over the top of the hill, then majestically sailed into a snowbank.

Folks who lived in Sullivan County were always prepared for winter problems, so after my breathing had returned to normal, I shoveled some of the snow, and with my pushing and Jean's rocking the car, we eventually got back to the road, went another half-mile, and parked the car. We walked to a friend's nearby farmhouse to spend the night.

That, too, will never be forgotten.

Judging by the tales I've heard about traffic accidents involving deer, we were very, very lucky.


## Accidents Involving Deer

According to data from the National Highway Traffic Safety Administration's Fatal Accident Reporting System,

*Warnings for the Road*

The following suggestions are not to be glanced over but committed to memory:

- When driving, be extra vigilant at dawn and dusk, the time of day when deer tend to travel.
- Pay attention to the side of the road.
- If one deer is present, there are probably more nearby.
- If you see deer, flash your headlights and honk the horn to scare them away from the road.
- If deer are in the road, do not take evasive action such as hard braking or swerving. If stopping is not possible, it is better to hit the deer than to cross the centerline or leave the road.

collisions with deer represent more than 4 percent of all crashes in the United States and in 1995 killed 111 people. The deer population jumped from approximately ten million in the 1980s to more than twenty million in 1995.

Although most deer- and other animal-related accidents do not involve human fatalities, more than sixteen thousand each year result in injuries, and more than 250,000 in damaged or totaled cars, adding up to more than $1 billion in insurance claims annually.

The problem is just as hazardous overseas. According to the Deer Commission for Scotland, in 1998, estimates of traffic accidents involving deer in the United Kingdom were between 20,000 and 42,000 a year, of which up to one-third are believed to have occurred in Scotland. These figures could be underestimates.

An article in the *Athens Daily News* in Athens, Georgia, reports the following: Motorists in Athens-Clarke County should beware when love-struck deer get more active in the autumn.

That's because Athens-Clarke's burgeoning growth has helped put it in the state's top ten in the number of deer–vehicle accidents three times since 1992: ninth in 1997 and 1995, and tenth in 1992.

In 1996, there were 8,539 reported accidents and 669 injuries, including two deaths. In 1997, accidents increased to 8,704, but injuries decreased to 643—again including two fatalities.

"More and more people are building houses where deer used to be," said Sgt. Howard Hensley of the state Department of Natural Resources.

Homeowners often plant new shrubbery in subdivisions, and heavier traffic along once-rural roads often compounds the problem.

Car-deer conflicts are also occurring in places like Columbia County, home to several Augusta suburbs. The fast-growing county ranked fourth among 159 Georgia counties in deer-vehicle accidents in 1997, said Gordy Wright, a spokesman for the Public Safety Department. Yet Columbia County barely makes the top fifty in deer population, according to Hensley.

Generally, areas like Columbia County support forty to forty-five deer per square mile—a typical number, said Haven Barnhill, a state Department of Natural Resources wildlife biologist.

"But with the increased development, you can have a lot more pushed into some areas, and, obviously, more conflicts," he said.

To reduce accidents, state authorities encourage hunters to harvest more deer.

Georgia hunters harvested 519,000 deer last year—up substantially from the previous year's harvest of 397,000. South Carolina hunters routinely harvest around 370,000 deer a year, but populations continue to grow.

South Carolina averages about 6,000 deer–vehicle accidents each year, causing more than four hundred injuries and spawning insurance claims that average $1,400 apiece, according to the South Carolina Insurance News Service.

*The Iowa City Press Citizen* reported that as the population of urban deer in Iowa City has increased, so have traffic accidents. In fact, the city recorded four times as many traffic accidents in 1999 as it did in 1996. Part of that increase is certainly because of motorists reporting more accidents— as the deer controversy has grown more public—but the city also credits the growing deer population.

Automobile accidents involving deer across North Carolina increased from 11,503 in 1998 to 12,233 in 1999, according to a University of North Carolina at Chapel Hill study. Deer caused 5.6 percent of all reported North Carolina driving accidents in 1999, up from 5.4 percent the previous year, the analysis of motor vehicle crash records showed. Reported mishaps involving deer grew by 6.3 percent over the twelve months, researchers said.

"From the many anecdotal reports we've received, these figures probably are just the tip of the iceberg when it comes to the real number of deer–motor vehicle crashes," said Dr. Donald Reinfurt, deputy director of the UNC Highway Safety Research Center. "That's because records are generated only when police officers write narratives about crashes and include the word 'deer.' When there's less than $1,000 damage and no injuries, which often is the case, the crashes are usually not reported at all."

It's interesting to note that western North Carolina, where I make my home, recorded relatively few deer crashes in 1999. The eastern counties showed the highest rates overall.

"Forty-two percent of North Carolina's deer crashes occurred down east, compared to 26 percent of the state's total number of crashes happening there," Reinfurt said. "Forty-nine percent of deer crashes were in the Piedmont, but there were a lot more here because more cars are on the roads. More than 60 percent of all North Carolina traffic accidents occurred in the Piedmont."

Dateline Wisconsin: Between 1983 and 1998, the number of car–deer crashes jumped from 28,269 to 41,829, an increase of 67 percent. During the same period, the size of the deer herd increased from 985,000 to one and a quarter million, an increase of 23 percent, while the number of vehicle miles driven on rural highways went up 58 percent from 17.9 billion miles to just over 30.8 billion.

And from Madison, Wisconsin—where the Office of the Commissioner of Insurance published tips for making sure your car is covered in case of an accident involving deer—comes the following:

"What we call 'collision insurance' does not cover physical damages that occur when a car hits a deer, so automobile owners should check to see if they've elected what's usually called 'comprehensive coverage,'" said Connie L. O'Connell, Commissioner of Insurance.

I called one of my local insurance agents (who did not want to be identified) about such accident insurance.

Insurance policies usually use one of two different terms to describe coverage that includes contact with animals: comprehensive coverage or other-than-collision coverage. Such coverage includes protection against damage to your vehicle that would be caused by hitting a deer, as well as damage from hail, theft, or falling objects. It is optional and includes its own deductible.

If their car hits a deer, a driver must have chosen medical payments coverage to be covered for bodily injuries. Medical payment coverage is offered at a certain dollar amount, usually a minimum of $1,000.

Drivers who are confused about their automobile insurance policies should call their insurance agents for further explanation.

*The Proper Placement of Deer Crossing Signs*

While searching for information about deer impact on traffic, I ran across the following information published by the Washtenaw County Road Commission of Ann Arbor, Michigan. I talked with Sheryl Soderholm Siddall, P. E., Supervisor of Traffic and Safety Engineering, who graciously gave me permission to reproduce the following:

The Michigan Manual of Uniform Traffic Control Devices lists Deer Crossing signs but it does not provide criteria for the installation and removal of these signs. Therefore, Washtenaw County Road Commission is defining criteria to be used in the installation and removal of Deer Crossing signs.

A deer–car accident history should be looked up for the stretch of road in question. Installation of Deer Crossing signs is warranted if five deer–car-related accidents have occurred in a twelve-month period.

Placement of the signs should be reviewed every third year. . . . When the accident study shows that no deer–car-related accidents have occurred in the study area in a minimum of a twelve-month period, the sign may be removed at the discretion of Washtenaw County Road Commission.

## The Hornet Deer Whistle

The Hornet Deer Whistle is a small, electrically powered generator that produces a high-powered, directional sonic wave. This wave can be tracked at 1,600 feet and has demonstrated the ability to alert deer and most other animals of an approaching vehicle with sufficient time and distance to avoid hitting the deer. Find it at www.deer-whistles.com.

## Nurseries and Gardens

The life of a nursery owner forced to continually think about and plan for deer invasions was summed up for me by Mark Pitts, owner of the Fantastic Plants Nursery in suburban Memphis, Tennessee.

Fantastic Plants is a small family mail-order business dealing with trees, shrubs, and perennials, including some new, unusual, and sometimes rare Japanese maples and conifers.

According to Mr. Pitts, deer generally leave the maples alone, but:

> If they are hungry, they eat anything. And we have real trouble when there's a hard frost or deep snow. We are close to the woods and they are soon within the bounds of the nursery. They go for anything perennial and soft.
>
> And it's not only deer. A few years ago, rabbits were locked in the greenhouse, and before we knew what happened, they ate a whole crop to the

ground. It's lucky for us that a lot of our plants are under glass or in cold frames for the winter and only uncovered in the summer when we can watch.

I called my old friend Kate Jayne at Sandy Mush Herb Nursery in Leicester, North Carolina, and asked her about protecting the many hostas they grow at their nursery.

Kate thought for a moment, then in her always-pleasant voice said, "If we didn't have four dogs, mutts that roam free, by the end of the spring we wouldn't have a hosta left—not only for the trade but for our own gardens as well!"

## The Private Town of Biltmore Forest

The town of Biltmore Forest is about three miles from Asheville, North Carolina. It supports its own police department, mayor, and city council, and is listed as one of the richest towns in North Carolina. According to the 2000 Census, Biltmore Forest has a per capita income of more than $85,000. It covers an area of 1,910 acres, land that was sold by Mrs. George Vanderbilt to a private company in 1920 for the purpose of developing an area for personal residences. The population is about 1,350 people, and untold numbers of deer.

Biltmore Forest is an enclave, its acres surrounded by roadways that act as moving fences to keep the deer within the following boundaries: To the north, the City of Asheville and one of the busiest Interstates in the Southeast, I-40; to the east, the five-lane Route 25, the Hendersonville Road, and I-240; to the south, the Blue Ridge Parkway, the bumper-to-bumper Long Shoals Road, and the four-lane Airport Road; to the west, I-26 and the French Broad River.

In July, 2002, a story appeared in the *Asheville-Citizen Times*:

"Biltmore Forest still aiming for shooters to kill deer in town." The story concerns town officials meeting with North Carolina Wildlife Resources Commission's Big Game Committee to mull over the town's hiring of Connecticut-based White Buffalo, Inc. to bait and shoot the deer. White Buffalo's Web site bills them as the leading experts in control of white-tailed deer, especially in suburban communities, city parks, and enclaves where deer outnumber human residents. They are listed as a non-profit agency. The town proposed hiring White Buffalo, but the commission rejected the proposal.

Earlier in the year, Richard Hamilton, deputy director of the commission, said the population control method "is inconsistent with our policy of controlling deer numbers through more conventional and less controversial methods." The commission suggested alternatives, including using plants that deer won't eat and putting up barriers between the town and the Biltmore Estate, where the deer roam. A fence would be too expensive and "unsightly," would cost between $300,000 and $400,000, and would have to be eight feet high, he said.

But the pressure is building to allow just such a solution.

Others have entered the fray, insisting that a fence around Biltmore Forest would do the job of keeping the deer out; others say the fence would not be high enough at eight or even ten feet to do the job. Although in some places a fourteen-foot fence is necessary, in the area of Biltmore Forest, with lots rather than open meadows, a ten-foot fence might work. But it could cost $500,000.

There are, of course, other possible solutions. I talked to Mayor Ramona Rowe about letting homeowners have their own fences, so if you had a garden you could protect your plants but if you wanted to opt out of a fence and invite deer into your yard, you could.

"Sure, deer are a problem," said the mayor, "but it's been a problem for a long, long time. And as long as I'm mayor, Biltmore Forest will not be a walled compound. Remember, Frederick Law Olmsted, the original landscape designer of the area, wanted this to be a residential area with a natural setting including trees and open spaces. We would like to remain fairly true to that concept. Although it's gone unnoticed by the media, we have relaxed ordinances for fencing side- and backyards. And we are still considering front-yard fencing. We have the option of electric fencing, too. But as to the solving the problem, we're a long way from that."

The debate in Biltmore Forest is, I suspect, the same debate that occurs across the country when a segment of the society wants to control wildlife.

I contacted Dr. Tony DeNicola, the director of White Buffalo, Inc. (WBI) about their potential contract to help Biltmore Forest.

"After all, it's a philosophical question," said Dr. DeNicola, "over the most humane methods to kill deer. Is it starvation, or their being injured by hitting cars or trucks, or using our sharpshooters who bait selected spots with corn, then shoot the deer from elevated locations, aiming for their head?

"In fact, sometimes we use drop nets to trap animals and captive bolt guns for killing. Then the meat is donated to charities.

"And," he added, "let me put the fence issue to rest." He explained further:

> Typically, suburban deer use an area of one hundred to three hundred acres. A recent study from Hilton Head, South Carolina, demonstrated that deer in a suburban development had "home ranges" of one hundred to one hundred fifty acres. Deer home ranges overlap considerably, so even though each individual will use one hundred to one hundred fifty acres, many deer can reside in a square-mile area (for example, there were over one hundred deer per mile squared in the Hilton Head study area).
>
> There are 640 acres in a square mile, so you can see how many of the deer in Biltmore Forest (1,451 acres) are truly resident animals, not Estate animals. Therefore, most of the deer in town do not travel onto the Estate (or vice versa).
>
> In the study from Hilton Head, they reduced a local population on roughly a square-mile area by

one-half and did nothing to the herd immediately adjacent to it on a mile squared. None of the deer from the unthinned herd moved into the thinned area. The only behavioral response was that the deer in the reduced density neighborhood used a slightly bigger home range. Deer began using an additional twenty to thirty acres after there were lower densities.

This clearly demonstrates that the placement of a fence would accomplish very little (i.e., deer from the Estate are not going to "fill the void" created by management efforts in town). . . .

Deer are very strongly tied to their home ranges and attempts to push them from these ranges will result in deer looping back upon any opportunity. So any attempt to "drive" deer onto the Estate would be very difficult. Looking at the logistics, one would need to form a line of people across the entire length of the town. This is approximately three miles. You would have to distribute people about ten yards apart to minimize the likelihood of deer breaking back through the line of people. There are 1,760 yards in a mile. This results in 176 people per mile or 528 people in a line for a "drive" of the town.

Think about trying to orchestrate such an endeavor: First, trying to get that many people available at one time would be nearly impossible. Second, there are areas of town that are densely vegetated (one would have to crawl through on their hands and knees). It would be very difficult to maintain the line of people without deer using these areas to double back through. Therefore, the probability of getting a significant number of deer through openings in the fence that they will not know the location of, is very low. Also, respect that once deer get cornered against the fence they will panic, and someone may get seriously injured as deer try to exit back through the line of people.

Of course, many residents of many communities disagree with Dr. DeNicola, including Chuck Rice, the executive director of the North Carolina Wildlife Federation, who said, "My biggest objections have to do with what I consider the ethics of the methods proposed."

Other residents of the town dislike the hunt idea, as well as proposals made for bow hunters (who would make less noise) instead of rifle bearers.

"There must be more reasons for a community to hire you than merely thinning out the herd," I said to Dr. DeNicola. "What are they?"

"Well, in addition to the cost of vehicle collisions and rising insurance costs, there is damage to landscapes both public and private, not to mention damage to the local ecology."

"But there must be steps you must follow?" I asked.

"Initially, it's necessary to have a public meeting so private landowners can understand what's involved in a euthanasia program," Dr. DeNicola explained. "First, deer distribution is assessed, then access to private properties, and finally, safe shooting in the selected areas. A baiting program is established to herd the deer and bring them to these areas. Shooting lanes are then cleared to ensure that there are no obstructions in the trajectory of the bullet. Patterns of human activity like dog walking, school bus routes, and joggers are noted, so that when the shooting begins we have maximum safety and, I might add, a sense of discretion.

"For each site, we select one of eleven specialized weapon systems each designed for select site characteristics. This decision is dependent on maximum shooting range, acceptable noise, proximity to homes, and deer abundance. Deer are euthanized with a single shot to the head, ensuring a humane kill."

"How does WBI maintain objectivity when communities are in the decision-making phase?" I asked.

"We simply review all available deer management options and then determine what is involved logistically: the costs, time frame, and compatibility with the local human activity. This information is then passed on to the powers that be so they can make a more informed decision."

"Can WBI implement a control program after an area has been hunted?" I asked.

"After being pursued by recreational hunters, it's difficult to professionally manage a deer population," he replied. "Prior to management actions, suburban deer are usually easy to approach. Deer that do not readily exhibit alarm behavior can be effectively and efficiently manipulated for the purposes of either capture, anti-fertility agents, or what we call 'remote euthanasia.' If deer are hunted, they become wary of the threat that humans pose, and any subsequent efforts to manage deer using similar techniques, like tree stands, are often compromised. The only cost-effective way to manage deer effectively uses methods that substantially differ from regular hunting. For example, approaching deer with a vehicle usually remains a viable option."

I asked about trapping and relocating deer.

Dr. DeNicola said that relocation of animals requires trapping, netting, and possibly remote chemical immobilization, always by experienced personnel. Costs can range from $400 to $2,931 per animal. Suitable release sites are necessary but often difficult to find. Relocating deer can result in stress-related death or disease transmission, like Lyme disease or tuberculosis. Once an animal is trapped, you must have experienced personnel so the handling procedures minimize stress and post-release death."

"I remember last year there was talk of Biltmore Forest using fertility control to keep the deer population at manageable levels. What is fertility control?" I asked.

"Fertility control," he answered, "is the ideal solution. Unfortunately, fertility control agents are currently not available for managing overabundant deer populations. You must realize that the Food and Drug Administration strictly regulates all the field studies and further research is required to review the feasibility and practicality of using contraceptives. Fertility control agents exist that can prevent reproduction in individual deer, but the need for repeated administration and limited delivery technologies reflect current problems. Data collected to date racks up a cost of manpower and materials equal to $1,000 per doe. That suggests that contraceptives will be limited to smaller herds."

"So with both relocation and fertility control being so expensive, a community like Biltmore Forest has just three options: sharpshooting, controlled hunting, and trapping linked to euthanasia," I said.

"That's right. The American Veterinary Medical Association approved sharpshooting as a humane form of euthanasia. Sharpshooting requires trained personnel to use a variety of techniques to maximize safety, discretion, and efficiency. This method is often implemented in suburban and urban settings with access to both public and private lands. Costs range from $91 to $300 per deer. Typically, all meat harvested is donated to area food shelters for distribution.

"Next is controlled hunting. Unfortunately, using hunters to manage overabundant deer populations often requires an approval from a state agency and law enforcement involvement, because there's the potential for animal welfare groups to become involved. Costs range from $162 to $622 per deer harvested, depending on the manpower required. Archery is another discreet removal technique but results in a lower success rate, because limited shooting ranges require a longer time frame of operation. Where feasible, firearms can be used to maximum efficiency.

"Finally, trapping and euthanasia are available for areas where there's a concern about, or a law prohibiting, the discharge of firearms. Physical restraints like box traps, clover traps, drop nets, or rocket nets are followed by euthanasia using a gunshot or captive bolt to the head. As mentioned above, deer are subjected to great amounts of stress during the restraint operation. The minimum cost is $400 per deer."

As of September 2002, the debate continues.

# 4

# *The Wonderful World of Fencing*

W hen installing a fence around your garden or property, think long-term. If you are not a dedicated gardener, or you plan to retire to Florida in a year or two, perhaps installing an expensive fence is not the best idea. After all, a good fence is not a cheap solution.

And to make your investment pay, it must be a good fence, carefully planned, specifically designed for your site, and installed with care and precision. Consider fencing as a long-term investment. A well-maintained fence should last between five and twenty-some years, depending on the type. Most fences pay for themselves within a few years by reducing deer damage.

When researching this book, I was amazed at how many Web sites and organizations suggested a six-foot fence for protecting a garden. Any healthy adult deer can easily leap six feet without ever breathing heavily. Most healthy deer can easily clear an eight-footer.

Given enough room and the knowledge of where they will land, there are many deer able to vault over a ten-footer. Here in Asheville we have the North Carolina Arboretum, carefully surrounded by a ten-foot-high wire fence. Because of dips and rises in the terrain in places, it is not high enough.

Deer are careful creatures. They will not purposefully put their lives in danger. So in a backyard situation, with limited open space for a deer to land, you might get by with an eight-foot fence. Their caution always works in your favor—deer will not jump without knowing they will safely land on the other side of any barrier.

And how about packed snow? If you live in an area with high snowfall and the kind of temperatures that turn snow into solid blocks of ice, then you need to add a foot to your fence for each foot of snow depth.

How about the driveway? I've seen people quarantine their property with an eight-foot fence, then block the driveway with a gate, only to leave the gate open because somebody forgot to close it.

Remember, a twelve-inch gap is enough for a deer to squeeze through. And the fence must be pegged or attached to the ground. I have seen an adult deer bend its legs and literally crawl under a chicken-wire fence. *Agile* is the word for deer.

## Non-Electric Fences

Today there are two basic types of fencing: non-electric and electric. Let's start with the non-electric varieties.

I remember when first protecting our Sullivan County garden, we had acquired about one hundred wooden bunk beds, because part of our property had once been a summer camp for kids. The beds were sturdily made, with mattress supports consisting of long metal straps attached to the frames.

Until we surrounded the garden with chicken wire held to wooden posts, we made a fence with two rows of bunk beds, one piled on top of the other. It certainly wasn't pretty, but it worked.

In situations where deer pressure is moderate to high and your garden means a lot to you, fencing becomes a necessity. Remember, you must begin with an eight-foot fence to exclude deer. Many designs of electric and non-electric fence are available to meet specific needs, whether it's a garden, nursery, or tree plantation. They range in cost from pennies per foot to as much as six dollars or more per linear foot.

One last thing: Remember to check local zoning laws, especially if you live in a town or a village. It would be a shame to go to the effort and expense of installing a fence only to find out it's illegal.

## Wire Mesh Fencing

It's with great pleasure that I credit an article entitled "Controlling Deer Damage in Missouri," agricultural publication MP685, November 1, 1997, by Robert A. Pierce II and Ernie P. Wiggers at the School of Natural Resources,

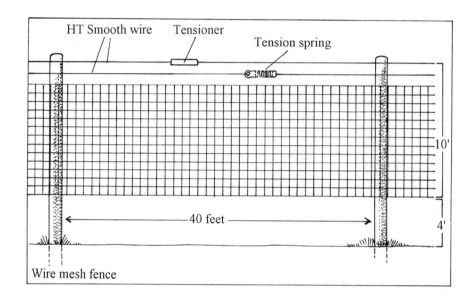

for much of the following information on the types of fences available today.

Woven-wire fences are used for year-round protection of high-value crops subject to high deer pressures. While expensive and difficult to construct, they are easy to maintain and highly effective. Woven-wire fences are assembled from two tiers of four-foot woven wire strung together to form an eight-foot barrier. The fence must be tight to the ground so deer are unable to crawl underneath. Other designs include six-foot woven wire with strands of high-tensile wire above that to a height of eight to ten feet. Little maintenance is required.

## Plastic Mesh Fencing

Non-electric plastic mesh fencing has great residential landscape applications. This type of fencing is lightweight, high-strength, and virtually invisible, so it does not detract from the appearance of the property it protects. The fencing consists of a seven-and-a-half-foot black plastic mesh with a life expectancy of ten years. This type of fence can be attached to existing trees or hung on pressure-treated posts. The lightweight material minimizes the need to install many posts. Twelve-inch white streamers are attached four feet off the ground and about a foot apart, to warn deer of the barrier. Galvanized twelve-inch stakes secure the fencing to the ground every twelve feet.

## Electric Fencing

Electric deer fences are the most common and effective type of fencing. They do their job because deer, unless chased, prefer to go through or under a fence rather than attempt to jump it. Electric fences are powered by high-voltage, low-impedance chargers, which provide timed pulses (forty-five to sixty-five per minute) of short duration (0.0003 seconds). How well a charger performs depends on its power output measured in joules (a unit of energy) under load.

Because deer hair is hollow, it's an effective insulator, and deer's small and pointed hooves also lessen the impact of an electric shock. Therefore, the type of fence charger used to deter cattle often lacks sufficient output to stop deer.

When selecting a charger, a good rule of thumb is one joule of output per 3,000 feet of fence wire. By determining the perimeter of your fenced area and the number of wires that will be charged, you can get a rough idea of your charger needs.

Also, unless you live in the middle of the North Woods with no chance of a stranger ever walking by your property, all electric fences must be marked with warning signs.

Chargers can be AC-powered, battery-charged, or solar-powered, and should maintain a charge greater than 5,000 volts on several miles of fence. It's best to use AC-powered chargers, because they have the lowest cost per joule of output and are the most reliable. A power wire can be run to the fence, or aluminum fence wire can be run considerable distances on posts from an AC-powered charger to the remote fence location. The cost of running a well-maintained electric fence with a four-joule energizer for one year is equivalent to the cost of running a 40-watt light bulb for one year. Battery chargers are adequate but must be properly maintained. Solar chargers have a solar panel that keeps a battery charged, but they are expensive and high-joule units must be custom made. In addition, solar chargers need the sun, and without adequate sunlight, they will fail.

## Fence Maintenance and Effectiveness

Just like taking care of a lawnmower or remembering to inflate car tires, after the first year many landowners experience problems with deer penetrating fences because they forget maintenance. Fences must be maintained to remain effective.

Whether using herbicides or cutting back by hand, vegetation must be kept off of the lower fence wires to reduce grounding and voltage loss. Voltage must be regularly checked and broken strands quickly repaired. Remember, deer will constantly test the fence, and if they are able to penetrate because the power is off or for some other reason, the fence will lose its effectiveness. A common mistake is forgetting to electrify the fence before leaving the area during construction or afterward.

During the off-season, some people have mistakenly turned off the power while leaving the fence in place. This renders the fence ineffective even after it is re-electrified, because the deer have learned that they can penetrate it. Fences used for temporary protection should be dismantled during the off-season. It's important to understand that most fences are not true physical barriers but behavioral barriers. The electric shock conditions the deer to stay away. Once deer know they can penetrate a fence, its effectiveness is seriously reduced.

Another problem is not providing a ten- to fifteen-foot cleared buffer outside the fence so deer can see the fence. On steep slopes this buffer must be wider. Without these buffers, deer will run into the fence, breaking it or going right through.

## Temporary Electric Fencing

Temporary electric fences provide inexpensive protection for many gardens, large or small. They are easy to construct, do not require rigid corners, and use readily available materials. The fences are designed to attract attention and administer a strong but harmless electric shock (high voltage, low amperage) when a deer touches the fence with its nose. Deer soon become conditioned to avoid these fences.

Such fences are easily installed and removed. The major cost associated with temporary electric fencing is the fence charger. Install the fence at the first sign of damage to prevent deer from establishing feeding patterns in your crops. Such fences require weekly inspection and maintenance.

## The Peanut Butter Fence

The peanut butter fence takes advantage of the fact that most animals like peanut butter. This fence is an effective but inexpensive construction, best used for gardens or nurseries subject to moderate deer pressures.

A single strand of 17-gauge wire is suspended about thirty inches above the ground by four-foot fiberglass rods at thirty- to sixty-foot intervals. Wood corner posts provide support. Flags of aluminum foil (4″ × 4″ squares folded over the wire) are attached to the wire at twenty- to fifty-foot intervals, held in place with tape or paper clips. Aluminum flashing can also be used and has the advantage of not being easily damaged or blown off.

Closer spacing may be necessary near existing deer trails and during the first few months the fence is used, as

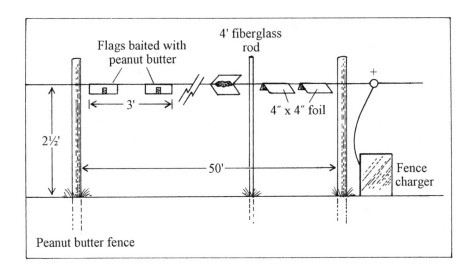

Peanut butter fence

you attempt to modify deer behavior. The underside of the flags is baited with a one-to-one mixture of peanut butter and vegetable oil. The smell attracts the deer, which touch or sniff the flags and receive an electric shock. The flags should be re-baited every four to eight weeks, depending on weather conditions.

## A Polywire and Polytape Fence

The original peanut butter fence can be greatly enhanced using polywire or polytape, rather than 17-gauge wire. Polys have the advantage of being more visible to deer, especially at night. They are also easier to roll up and remove. Polywire has a life expectancy of five to seven years.

Polywire is composed of three, six, or nine strands of metal filament braided with strands of brightly colored polyethylene. A wider polytape is available and has the added advantage of being stronger and more visible—but it's also more expensive. Although both polywire and polytape come in a variety of colors, many users claim that white provides the greatest contrast to most backgrounds and is the easiest for deer to see, especially at night. The loss of voltage over long distances of polywire/polytape can be a problem, so purchase materials with the least electrical resistance (ohms per 1,000 feet).

In its simplest application, an electrified single strand of polywire is suspended about thirty inches above the ground by four-foot fiberglass rods at twenty- to fifty-foot intervals and baited in the same way as the original peanut butter fence. A second wire can be added to increase effectiveness: one wire placed eighteen inches above the ground and the other at thirty-six inches above the ground. This prevents fawns from walking under the fence and also increases the chance that one wire will remain electrified if deer knock the fence over.

Usually only the top wire is baited. In smaller areas, such as home gardens, more wires can be added on taller poles if desired, and closely spaced bottom wires can keep out rabbits and woodchucks. It's always important to clear vegetation under the fence so it does not short out.

Fiberglass rods do not provide enough support for use as corner posts. At corners, it's better to use four-foot metal fence stakes with a bottom plate that provides stability when it is pounded into the ground. A piece of thin-walled, one-inch PVC pipe can be slipped over the metal stake to act as an insulator, with the polywire or polytape

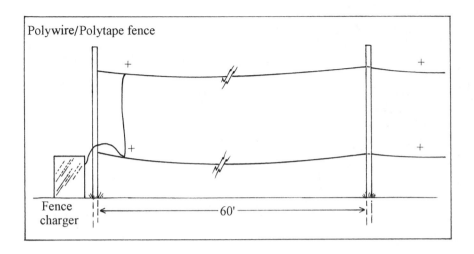

Polywire/Polytape fence

Fence charger

60'

wrapped around it a few times. This allows the stringing of the wire with sufficient tension to hold the flags. A variety of wooden posts with plastic insulators will also work.

The use of electric fences around homes often causes concern for the safety of children and visitors. One option is to put the fence charger on a timer, so it turns on from dusk to dawn.

## Permanent and Semi-Permanent Electric Fencing

High-tensile fencing can provide year-round protection from deer damage. Many designs are available to fit specific needs. All require strict adherence to construction guidelines concerning rigid corner assemblies and fence configurations. Frequent inspection and maintenance are necessary. High-tensile fences have a twenty- to thirty-year life expectancy.

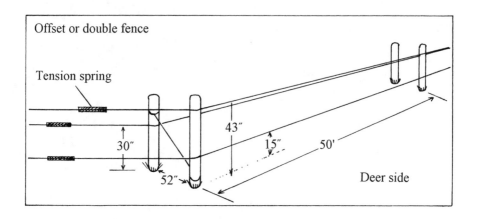

Offset or double fence

Tension spring

30″

43″

15″

50′

52″

Deer side

## The Offset or Double Fence

Here's an effective fence design best suited for gardens, nurseries, or truck farms under forty acres in size. The fence's electric shock coupled with its three-dimensional design repel the deer. More wires can be added if deer pressures increase.

## A Vertical Electric Deer Fence

Here's a permanent fence for protecting large truck gardens, orchards, and other fields from moderate to high deer pressures. It offers highly effective protection for areas up to twenty-five acres. A wide variety of fence materials and specific designs are available, including variations in the number of wires (five, seven, nine, or more) and fence height (five to ten feet). Posts are usually driven into the ground and high-tensile, 12-gauge wire is applied and maintained under high tension—hence the need for good support.

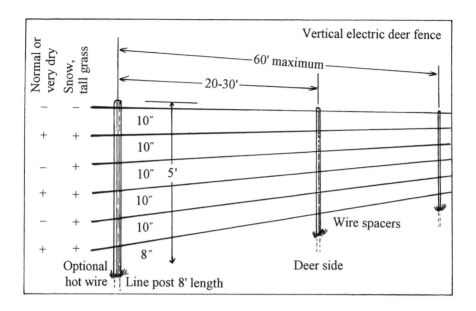

A high-voltage, low-impedance, New Zealand-style charger powers this fence. Because of the prescribed wire spacing, deer try to go through the fence and are effectively shocked. Vertical fences use less ground space than three-dimensional fences, but are probably less effective at keeping deer from jumping over. I recommend that you employ a local fence contractor.

**A Slanted Seven-Wire Fence**

This fence differs from the vertical fence in both post alignment and wire barrier. It's constructed at a thirty-degree angle to the ground with the result that a deer must carefully consider the jump. Its three-dimensional design (five feet high by eight feet wide) and electric shock present a formidable barrier. It's used primarily

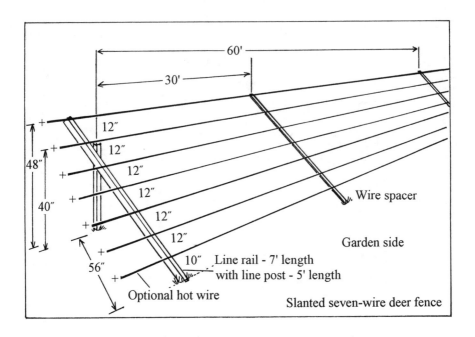

where high deer pressures threaten moderate-sized to large orchards, nurseries, and other high-value crops.

Construct the fence using 12-gauge wire. The wires are attached to slanted fence battens at fifty-foot intervals to achieve the three-dimensional effect. One drawback to this fence is that it requires eight feet of space along its entire length, which increases maintenance costs.

### The Electric Spider Fence

The spider fence is a relatively new fencing concept that combines multi-wire electric fencing technology with medium cost and offers good protection. This five-wire fence is four feet tall and uses a 17-gauge wire, not held un-

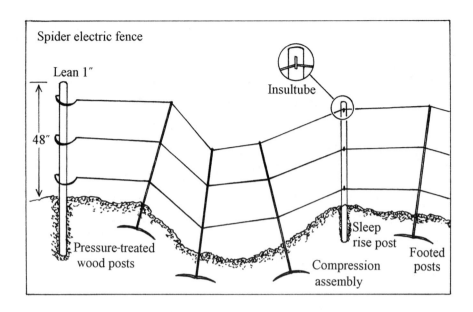

der high tension. The only driven posts are the corners, and intermediate fiberglass posts are used periodically to maintain wire spacing and height. Minimal wire tension is increased or decreased by wrappings on the Spider G-Spring at the gate opening system. Because there are few driven posts and low tension, the fence is semi-permanent and much cheaper to construct than conventional high-tension systems. Baiting with peanut butter flags, described earlier, is essential to make this fence effective. Properly maintained, this fence has a life expectancy of ten to twelve years.

## Some Fencing Sources

Before ordering heavy-duty fence supplies from across the country, look in your Yellow Pages and check for fence

dealers in your area. The following companies sell all sorts
of protective fences:

- **Benner's Gardens** (www.deerfencedirect.com) sells a
  number of deer fences made of a patented ultravio-
  let-light-resistant polypropylene that can be fixed to
  posts or wrapped around or drawn between trees in
  wooded areas. Its sister company, Deer Fencers, has
  installation crews based in New York, New Jersey,
  Connecticut, Pennsylvania, Delaware, Maryland, Virginia, Illinois, Wisconsin, North Carolina, Massachusetts, Maine, and Rhode Island. They also have
  California-based crews that cover areas from Monter-
  rey to the Napa Valley, including the Bay Area and
  the Sierra foothills. Deer Fencers can be reached at
  1–800–BIG–DEER. If your property is located in another region, they most likely can provide you with
  the names and numbers of contractors experienced
  with installing their fencing. Call Benner's Gardens
  at 1–800–753–4660.
- **Gallagher Power Fence** (www.gallagherusa.com) system gives deer a short, sharp, but safe shock they
  won't forget. The most powerful Gallagher Energizer
  has the capacity to power long distances of multi-wire
  fence. This has spread the use of electrical fencing
  on to large properties and enabled the control of
  wild animals. Their Web site has the following impressive information: Gallagher Power Fences have
  kept elk off golf courses in Montana and Oregon,

blue herons out of crayfish ponds in Louisiana, raccoons out of sweet-corn patches all over the Midwest, bears out of beehives from Montana to Maine, sea lions off boat docks in California, moose off railroad tracks in Alaska, squirrels out of pecan orchards in California, deer out of flowerbeds and vineyards from Vermont to Virginia, and coyotes and mountain lions out of calving pastures across the country.

- **Gardener's Supply Company** (www.gardeners.com) markets an Easy-Up Fence that can be attached to posts or stakes to create a quick, temporary fence. At season's end, simply roll it back up. Once in place, the seven-foot high, black, five-eighth by three-quarter-inch mesh netting is almost invisible. Made of tough, UV-stabilized polypropylene for years of seasonal use, it can be cut in half easily with scissors for a shorter fence, and can also be wrapped around shrubs.

- **Havahart Electronic Repellent** (www.havahart.com) for deer attracts deer to posts with a lure scent—harmlessly repelling deer from your yard or garden. The system includes three posts covering approximately one thousand square feet. It is easy to assemble and install. Natural garden colors allow this product to blend into your garden or yard. Electronics are impervious to cold, heat, and rain for year-round control. Extensive field-testing backed by research has proven this product to be effective.

Repellent delivers four hundred volts (substantially less than a static shock) with virtually no amps (0.1 joules). This will harmlessly repel deer and is completely safe for pets and people.

Havahart reports this method is **very effective** in suburban areas where deer density is low, and damage is mild, infrequent, and unpredictable; **effective** in areas where deer density is medium, and damage is moderate, frequent, and predictable; **effective** (if repellent is moved as deer travel patterns change) in rural, residential areas where deer density is medium to high, and damage is extensive, frequent, and predictable; and **not effective** in rural, non-residential, agricultural areas where deer density is high, and damage is extreme, frequent, and unpredictable.

- **Not Here Deer®** (www.notheredeer.com) greatly reduces the extent of deer damage by emitting an ultrasonic signal specially designed to repel deer. While it is harmless to the animal, it creates sound distortions that prohibit the deer from effectively using its keen auditory system for predator detection. Deer become anxious, then retreat to an area outside the unit's range.

- **Romancing the Woods, Inc.** (www.rtw-inc.com) is a corporation in Woodstock, New York, that designs and sells various gates, pergolas, and fences for keeping deer out. The styles are researched and finished in the grand manner of nineteenth-century parks and gardens, and in the style of the Adirondack

Great Camps. Everything they create is custom designed and constructed to your specific requirements, and available in any length and height.
Indestructible eastern red cedar is used throughout.

## *Tree Shelters*

- I first ran across tree shelters while walking in a
  meadow adjacent to the Pink Beds, a glorious site
  maintained by the U.S. Forest Service, not far from
  the Blue Ridge Highway. It's the sort of place where
  deer roam free and with impunity.
- **Tubex® Treeshelters** (www.treessentials.com) surround saplings, encasing each plant within a plastic
  tube. The transparent, corrugated polypropylene
  tubes are placed around seedlings at the time of
  planting. Tubex tubes are each supported by one
  $1'' \times 1''$ wooden stake pounded into the ground next
  to the shelter. An ultraviolet inhibitor is added to the
  polypropylene to prevent it from breaking down too
  rapidly when exposed to sunlight. Shelters normally
  disintegrate after seven to ten years.

  A four-foot shelter is generally used and prevents
  deer from browsing on seedlings. A five-foot shelter
  may be needed in areas with excessive browsing or
  snowfall. In addition, the shelter also acts like a
  miniature greenhouse and promotes fast growth of
  the protected plant. These shelters are used mostly in
  forestry applications to protect hardwood tree

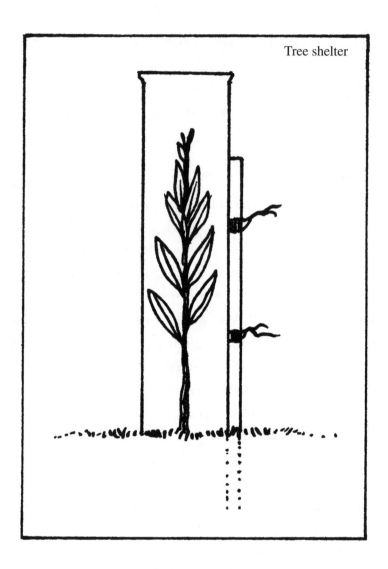

Tree shelter

seedlings, with up to one hundred shelters per acre. Larger shelters are also available. The shelters also make it easy to apply herbicides for weed control. Tubes are available in two-, three-, four-, and five-foot sizes.

# 5

# Solutions on Your Own

We covered the pros and cons of fencing in Chapter Four, but there are other ways to control deer. Here are some of the mechanical methods available for today's gardens.

## Scaring Devices

Deer can be frightened just as easily as you. They hate an unexpected loud noise, they find many smells offensive, and they abhor flashing lights—but frankly, unless far from your home, in order to be effective these will probably annoy you, too. Deer also do not like roaming dogs or the smell of dogs.

## Dogs Around the Yard

As long as we lived in Sullivan County, we had a dog. Our first dog was a vishlu, a great animal—a bit flaky, but fun to have around. If Zoltan walked the property in the early morning, at noon, in the late afternoon, and in the evening, we had few problems.

But in the winter, with a lot of snow on the ground, Zoltan was not perfect, especially as he was well-trained and not allowed to run the deer. And they soon learned that here was one dog who barked but never chased. That meant the garden around the house was pretty safe from deer, but the outlying sections were still under threat.

Now here I must interject something that Jean and I did to protect our Sullivan County garden:

By the beginning of the 1980s, I was earning the majority of our living by writing garden books, and I tried to grow many of the plants I wrote about.

But we had no way of fencing thirty-three acres, and our house and garden sat about a tenth of a mile back from the main road. So the entire front area, totaling about six acres, was free for the deer to roam.

Zoltan did a good job around the house, but beyond a certain perimeter, he failed.

We tried everything, including having New York friends (male, and meat-eaters) relieve their bladders (discreetly, of course) at the edge of the garden. It didn't work.

We played radios (apparently works for some), with music from rock to Bach, but it never deterred the deer (maybe the volume wasn't loud enough, but we lived there, too).

We tried hanging tin cans and spirals of shiny aluminum, to no avail.

So we decided to feed the deer during the worst of the winter. After making arrangements with a local hunting club (they provided the cracked corn), Jean went out every day to an area down from the house and spilled a pail-full of corn upon the ground.

It didn't take long for the deer to accept her, and soon, following a precise pecking order, they ate the corn and left my dwarf conifers and roses alone.

Do not use hay, as it's bad for deer in the wintertime.

And in many states, feeding deer is against the law, so consult your local DEC or hunting clubs.

When Zoltan died, we went a year without a dog and were punished for it by an increase in garden invasions. So our next dog was a stray, a beautiful German shorthaired pointer called Bismarck. In conjunction with feeding the deer, Bismarck kept the damage to a reasonable level until we left the farm in 1989.

If you have a dog patrolling the garden, you are at an advantage. But I must make it clear that the dog must be trained not to run deer in the winter, especially when they are hungry, possibly starved.

One method of using a dog as a deer deterrent depends on the so-called 'invisible fence,' an electronic system whereby the dog wears a radio receiver in his collar that administers an electric shock if the dog gets too close to a perimeter wire attached to a transmitter.

## Renting Out Your Land

If you live in the country or near a park where hunting is allowed, and own a substantial amount of land, you might consider combining deer population control and recreational hunting.

You can invite hunters who are knowledgeable and trustworthy to use your land for the hunt.

Or you might decide to become a recreational hunter yourself.

Consider leasing your land to a local hunting club and develop a contract with clearly defined responsibilities. You might even barter the use of your land for some venison down the line.

## The Rube Goldberg Method

Rube Goldberg (1883–1970) was a Pulitzer Prize–winning cartoonist, sculptor, and writer who, over the years, developed a number of fantastic inventions in order to get something done on a comically convoluted level. He would put bells, whistles, gears, wires, weights, and live birds together in an imaginative way, for example, to wake somebody up without an alarm clock.

Today, the average home store stocks an incredible number of electronic devices that will turn lights on when a car, a person, a dog, and perhaps a mouse walks by the sensor. There are electric eyes that, if properly set in the garden, will not only give you an accurate pest count but again, turn on lights, whistles, recorded dog barks, or even explosions.

Be creative!

## Gas Exploders

Gas exploders and strobe light blinkers can be set around the garden's perimeter, but are not cheap solutions. The deer soon learn what to expect, so use these only as a short-term solution. To get the most out of this product, you must move the appliance and stagger the firing sequence.

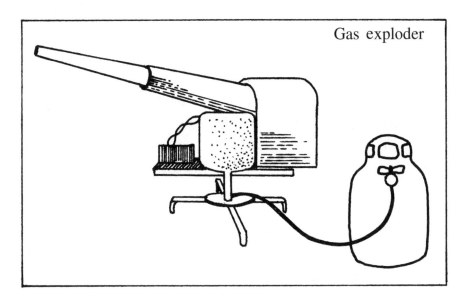

Gas exploder

### *Non-Commercial Repellents*

The number of repellents on the market today seem to be growing in step with the burgeoning deer populations, so they will be covered in Chapter Six. Here we deal with a few solutions that gardeners have devised using their own experiences and their own methods. But lay off the mothballs, as they are very detrimental to the environment.

## Human Hair

Human hair is one of those methods of repelling deer that many gardeners swear by and others write off as an urban legend. The suggestions are to obtain hair from a local beauty salon or barber shop, storing it in plastic bags until ready for use. Then place the hair in small mesh bags, nylon stockings, or panty hose. The bags should contain at least two hefty fistfuls of hair and be attached to plants at a height of twenty-eight inches to three feet, no more than three feet apart. Start hanging bags in early spring and replace them at least once a month. Some gardeners report increased success when occasionally spraying the bags with cologne or aftershave.

## Tankage

Various extension agents mention tankage as a deer repellent, so I include it here—although I would rather hire a watchman or build a high wall than use this method.

Tankage is a slaughterhouse byproduct traditionally used as a deer repellent in orchards where it repels deer by the smell, as would be obvious to anybody entering the garden. To prepare containers for tankage, remove the tops from aluminum pop cans, puncture the sides in the middle of the cans to allow for drainage, and attach them to the ends of four-foot stakes. Drive the stakes into the ground one foot from every tree you want to protect or at six-foot intervals around the perimeter of a block. Place one cup of tankage in each can.

## Soap

I'll bet you never thought when watching a soap commercial on TV that such a product might be used to repel deer! Again, it's possible that soap as a weapon might be an urban legend, but many gardeners swear that it works. Do not use expensive soap from a cosmetics counter but rather the kind that comes in plastic bags at discount stores. Drill a hole in each bar (you can use an electric drill or just a Phillips-head screwdriver), then suspend the soap with a stout length of cord from a nearby branch. Each bar appears to protect a radius of about one yard. Any inexpensive, tallow-based brand of bar soap will work. In addition to being an odor-based repellent, soap may reduce deer browsing as a visual cue—gardeners report that empty soap-bar wrappers alone have sometimes reduced damage.

## Meat-Eater's Urine

I mentioned this before, and lest you forget, we tried this one year up in Sullivan County. It did not work with local friends, but a number of New Yorkers, who are always interested in trying something new, were willing to try the following procedure (except in the winter). Various males were asked to relieve themselves at the far end of the garden, along an established line.

It doesn't work with vegetarians.

## Deer Scares from Japanese Gardens

And you think you've got problems! Back in the days when Japanese farmers battled the elements (and the animals) without the aid of electric fences and contemporary deer repellents, they fashioned the *shishi odoshi*, or the "deer scare," to frighten not only deer but wild boars, too.

Water travels through a thin bamboo pipe into a longer, and larger, bamboo pipe, which is set on an axle, with the first bamboo joint of the front end cut away as a type of spout and the bottom of the larger bamboo sealed.

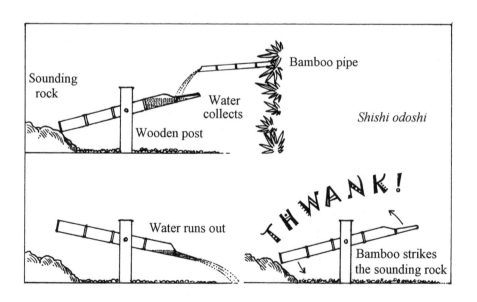

Sounding rock

Bamboo pipe

Water collects

Wooden post

Shishi odoshi

Water runs out

THWANK!

Bamboo strikes the sounding rock

The water collects in the bamboo and the weight forces the back end to tip to the ground. Then the continuing stream of water tips the pipe the opposite way and the water runs out the front. Now the back end is heavier than the front, and the pipe falls back to strike a large rock giving a loud *"Thwank!"* In addition to scaring deer, the flow of water and the regular movement of the *shishi odoshi* provide an effective counterpoint to the quiet permanence of the rest of a Japanese garden.

# 6

# *A Product Roundup*

Time was when calling a corporation "repellent" would have led to bad feelings, at least among the Board of Directors. But times change, and today environmentalism has become a way of life, if not with many corporations, at least with backyard gardeners. With that change in attitude, the world has traded buckshot and poison for products that shoo instead of kill, more humanely repellent to the animals involved.

A few rules of thumb:

1. Repellents do not eliminate browsing, only reduce it. Success with repellents is measured by your success in keeping browsing down to an acceptable level. If you cannot abide any damage, you must fence.
2. Some repellents stand up to weather better than others, and rainfall (or compacted snow) will wash off many repellents, so they must be reapplied.

3. Rarely will repellents stop deer from rubbing antlers.
4. Just like with teaching children, it's important to start early, before deer's feeding habits are established.
5. The availability of other food often determines the success of repellents.
6. One gardener's successful repellent is another gardener's failure, as the season, the time, the weather, and other factors can affect success or failure.
7. Stay informed, as new repellents and new formulas are appearing in astonishing numbers.

The following chemicals and products are on today's market. Whenever possible, I've given a description of their actions, and, because Web-business is growing by cyber-leaps, a Web site address. I have not covered all the products on the market. Some have disappeared, hopefully to resurface when sold to another company; some companies never market their product individually but sell directly to wholesalers, who then sell to retailers.

Most manufacturers note that their products work under most normal circumstances, but when deer are starving, they will often eat even things that are offensive.

- **Becker Underwood** (www.beckerunderwood.com) manufactures animal repellents using the term "aversion products." They have two offerings: Rejex It®, a bird repellent, and Tree Guard®, a deer repellent. These products are described as being environmentally friendly. Tree Guard is a blend of bittering agents and an odor detection compound linked with a binding agent, so the products continue to work long after a rainfall.

- **Bobbex Inc.** (www.bobbex.com) manufactures all natural deer repellents, organic plant growth stimulants, and chemicals for lawn treatments. Bobbex deer repellents coat foliage with a safe, non-chemical residue that they claim deer, smaller four-legged pests, and those horrors of the bird world, Canada geese, avoid like the plague.

- **Bonide Products, Inc.** (www.bonideproducts.com) manufacture Shotgun®, a formula that contains putrescent whole egg solids, garlic, and capsaicin, to protect flowers, shrubs, and trees from deer, rabbits, and squirrels, with both an odor and a taste challenge. Shotgun uses all natural ingredients and it leaves no noticeable residue.

- **Brookstone Deer Repellents** (www.brookstone.com) are hung or staked next to plants you'd like to protect. Deer can't stand its scent, so they won't trample beds, consume bulbs or flowers, or nip off delicate tree branches. This product keeps its strength through rain and snow for a full season, up to a year. It uses no chemicals or harmful ingredients. Each cube is tucked inside a sturdy mesh bag with a hanging loop.

- **Carnivore Urines** (www.predatorpee.com) or "predator pees," are a new branch of protective gardening featuring urines collected from bobcats, coyotes, foxes, and wolves. They work by sending a signal to all those animals out to prune your garden that a vicious, meat-eating animal is roaming the vegetable rows or that great display of bountiful flowers. The vented dispensers last for about thirty days and are filled with the urine solution of your choice. To get it right, consult the following:

  In the company's words, coyote urine is a powerful communicator. It attracts a coyote to its mate. It helps prey such as deer and other animals tell whether an area is safe or dangerous. It marks a coyote's territory and signals his dominance in the pack. Hunters, trappers, and others who interact with wild animals have long understood how animal urines can trigger instinctive reactions. This product is 100-percent real coyote urine and creates the illusion that coyotes are present. Deer, raccoon, and possum react instinctively in fear of this predator.

  Fox urine is powerful in the wild, repels woodchucks (groundhogs), rabbit, skunks, squirrel, and chipmunks. It also attracts a fox to its mate. It helps prey such as rabbits, groundhogs, skunks, squirrels, chipmunks, and other varmints tell whether an area is safe or dangerous. It marks a fox's territory and signals his dominance.

Bobcat urine stops moles, mice, and other small rodents by making them think bobcats are present. They react instinctively to their fear of the predator.

PredatorPee also makes Shake 'n Go Granules, solutions of bobcat, fox, and coyote urine. Again in the company's words: " . . . easy to use and the perfect solution for effective wide area coverage . . . just shake 'n go!"

- **Deer Blocker**® (www.pestproducts.com) is an all food-based product that contains putrescent egg, which emits the smell of animal proteins, plus garlic to confuse their sense of smell. Capsaicin, from peppers, contributes a burning sensation, which apparently deer hate. Dr. T, the manufacturer, also points out that applications do not change the color or texture of leaves and flowers.

- **Deer Busters.com** (www.deer-busters.com) carry many products, including Millers Hot Sauce®, a formula that repels deer, rabbits, and mice and is effective on fruits, nut trees, vegetables, vine crops, and ornamentals.

- **Deer No No**® (www.deernono.com) consists of a specially formulated citrus scent that apparently deer detest but which is pleasing to people. A solid cake is hung in a green-net bag and lasts up to twelve months. You have to hang a bag near the plant you wish to protect, about two feet or so apart. If the deer stop bothering a particular plant, you can remove the bag for future use.

- **Deer-Off®** (www.deer-off.com) was acquired by the Woodstream Corporation (they make Havahart Traps), which goes to show that fighting deer is a growing industry. Deer-Off is made of biodegradable food products that contain no harmful chemicals and are harmless to people—but deer, rabbits, and squirrels hate it. A single application lasts up to three months, although back home at the kitchen sink, it can be washed off fruits and vegetables. It won't dissipate from exposure to rain and snow, will not change the color or texture of plants, and does not leave a filmy residue. It should be noted that in a four-year study conducted by the Rutgers University Department of Animal Sciences, Deer-Off kept deer away from vegetation up to three times longer than the next most effective material.

- **Durapel®** (www.treessentials.com) is a pre-mixed, spray-on deer repellent that works by coating trees and plants with a white latex that gives up to five months of protection. The coating dries clear and is resistant to rain runoff and the effects of the sun. Only new growth needs to be protected after initial application. Durapel is safe for use around pets and will not harm plants or wildlife.

- **Hinder®** (www.protectyourgarden.com) is an easy-to-apply repellent with a smell disgusting to deer but not detectable to humans. It's also safe for applications on food or feed crops.

- **Hot Pepper Wax®** (www.hotpepperwax.com) is an environmentally friendly method of repelling moles and gophers from your lawn. The combination of castor oil, a wetting agent, and the convenience of a hose-end sprayer makes it easy to get the material into the soil, where it can immediately get to work.

- **Liquid Fence®** (www.liquidfence.com) is a biodegradable animal repellent made to keep animals, including deer, away from your garden. Based on odors that these animals find offensive, the formula is a non-toxic egg and garlic mix that lasts a full month before it must be renewed. It repels deer and rabbits from your shrubs, veggies, trees, and vines.

- **N.I.M.B.Y. or Not In My Back Yard** (www.nimby.com) is an emulsion of natural oils, blended to work with nature. Originally developed for the power utility industry, it has been tested in gardens and other sites throughout the United States and comes ready-to-use in a convenient 32-ounce trigger spray bottle. It's easy to apply, and one or two bottles should last the typical gardener most of the season. It can also be used on trashcans, bird feeders, and other areas.

- **Not Tonight Deer** (www.nottonight.com) is a powder which you mix with water and spray on the plants you want to protect. The deer are repelled by the smell of eggs. The pepper is a taste deterrent. Not Tonight Deer is not a perimeter repellent applied around the edge of your garden—you have to spray any plants you want protected from deer.

- **Outdoor Animal Repellents®** (www.champion.com) are billed as all-natural animal repellents for keeping pests away from garbage bags, digging in lawns, and ravaging flower beds, birdhouses, and the old compost heap. It reacts on an animal's senses of smell and taste and is effective against deer, raccoons, rabbits, squirrels, dogs, cats, and many other animals. These formulas pass the standards set by the Food Quality Protection Act and the EPA Office of Children Safety Protection. Outdoor Animal Repellents are in a liquid, ready-to-use form. They have a fresh lemon scent, making them non-offensive to humans.

- **Plant Pro-Tec®** (www.plantprotec.com) manufactures clip-on capsules lasting up to eight months. Developed by a forestry researcher, they take advantage of the deer's keen sense of smell. Easily concealed, these effective capsules use garlic oil to overpower and disrupt other scents that attract deer. Should a deer brave the smell and nibble, pepper oil in the capsule will change his mind. Capsules should be placed approximately every four feet and are sold in bags of twenty-five.

- **Plantskydd®** (www.treeworld.com) boasts bloodmeal as its main ingredient, as opposed to most other repellents that use egg-based formulas. But don't use it on flower blossoms, because it leaves a light red residue. Apparently this spray really sticks to plants and so remains effective even in severe rain or snow.

- **Repellex®** (www.repellex.com) is so bitter that, if you don't wear gloves when handling it and you get close to the liquid, you'll get a bitter taste in your mouth. This product is advertised as being effective against whitetails, mule deer, field mice, beavers, moose, moles, pocket gophers, rabbits, prairie dogs, porcupines, voles, and for good measure, grasshoppers. The Repellex people note that repellents won't stop deer from rubbing their antlers on trees to remove their velvet in the fall, although the odor may be strong enough to prompt the animals to choose another rubbing post.

- **Ro-Pel®** (www.ropel.com) is one of the worst-tasting substances ever known, according to the manufacturers. It tastes so foul—well, you know the old joke. Applications are said to be effective against raccoons, rats, deer, beavers, cats, rabbits, and woodpeckers (yellow-bellied sapsuckers) when sprayed on the target plants. You are warned not to taste it, lest it change your outlook on food forever.

- **Scare Wars®** (www.reedjoseph.com) uses radio and computer technology to operate a system of LP gas cannons that fire only on command. Scare Wars® is marketed as the finest bird and wildlife deterrent on the market today, because it only engages when there is a target in the sights. Birds and pests never grow accustomed to the cannon detonations, so the element of surprise is maintained each time the system is activated. I suspect this is not a system for small lots in the suburbs.

- **St. Gabriel Laboratories** (www.milkspore.com) is a commercial research lab founded by the Reuter Company in 1986. Their products include Hot Pepper Wax Animal, a compound used to repel animals from flowers and vegetables. Made from a blend of extremely hot cayenne pepper extracts combined with a food-grade wax, it will last even after rainfall. The company cites rabbits, tree squirrels, gophers, hedgehogs, prairie dogs, chipmunks, and more, but doesn't mention deer specifically. They also manufacture Ant, Flea & Tick Control, made from diatomaceous earth and pyrethrum (a natural product harvested from chrysanthemums) combined as the primary active ingredients to control numerous pests.

- **Tree Guard®** (www.bugpage.com) is a safe-to-use, pre-mixed, latex-based deer repellent that sprays on milky and dries clear. The active ingredient, Bitrex, makes the coated plant taste terrible. A detection agent lets deer know the plant is treated. Tree Guard leaves a clear sheen that resists rain and snow and can be used on any non-food plant; it won't harm deer, plants, people, or the environment. Where deer pressure is high, consider other abatement options including fencing.

- **Trident Enterprises International** (www.tridentent.com) offers a number of deer- and animal-repelling products. They include deer repellents; deer fencing (electric or non-electric invisible mesh barriers, and netting); scare devices that feature motion-activated, ultrasonic animal repellers; sonic animal repellers, including a motion-activated scarecrow that surprises deer (not to mention the neighbor's cat) with a blast of cold water when they trip the switch (Trident suggests this is an excellent repellent and a great way to move them out without having to reapply repellents); mole and gopher controls, featuring sonic repellers, mole and gopher repellents, or smoke bombs; squirrel controls; and animal detection devices, these last being cameras that photograph the invaders as they set off the secret trips, so you know exactly who is out to get you.

- **Weyerhaeuser Corporation**
  (www.Weyerhaeuser.com) developed Deer Away®, for use in reforestation projects to protect fir seedlings from deer damage. Since that time, it's proven effective in repelling rabbits and elk, too. The active ingredients in Deer Away are putrescent egg solids, an effective deterrent because of the acute sensibility of a deer's nose (hundreds of millions of odor receptors, as opposed to the human nose with its paltry five million). This potent mix is offensive to deer but not to people. An oil-based sticking agent keeps the product from washing off when it rains, but it must be applied to new growth and repeated after a heavy rain.

## Application of Commercial Repellents

The first application of a repellent should be within two weeks of plants or trees beginning to open buds. During the growing season, apply repellents whenever it's necessary to protect new growth—usually every month or so. With some crops it may be possible to disrupt deer feeding simply by spraying a wide strip on the border of the planting. For protection during the dormant season, mid-fall and early winter applications are recommended. Fall applications may help prevent antler-rubbing.

When using chemicals, no matter how benign their descriptions, always—I repeat, *always*—follow the manufacturer's instructions. All too often, I've watched gardeners figure that if one teaspoon per gallon makes an effective fertilizer compound, then doubling the mix will guarantee better results.

When applying liquids or powders, pick a calm day with no chance of imminent rain. This allows liquids to dry and set on the leaf surface. Never use repellents on anything that you plan to eat. If deer won't eat it, neither should you.

Always wear gloves when applying repellents, and don't touch your lips with your gloves.

# 7

# Plants Unpopular With Deer

Glancing through the following list of plants, I suspect even many seasoned gardeners will be surprised by the number of species ignored, shunned, or disliked by deer. Of course there are exceptions, but generally it's a safe bet to plant these species.

But I've said it before and I'll say it again: Deer are intelligent living creatures programmed by their genes and their history to survive over all surmountable odds. If starving, they will eat almost anything.

Any gardener who had to work with only the following plants would still find they had a garden of great beauty and should be reasonably happy with their lot.

It's also interesting to note just how many of the following plants are listed in various herbal and medicinal guides for their use in treating diseases and bodily discomforts. From the Native Americans to the early settlers to today's pharmacies, many of these native plants have been collected for use as drugs, poultices, herbal teas, and the like.

Many of these plants are bitter or have unpleasant textures or are highly purgative when eaten. And, unfortunately, smaller pests do not necessarily ignore a number of the following plants.

Since this chapter deals with gardens, let me remind you that a nursery bed is a great addition to any garden where potential pests are present. Such beds are out-of-the-way spots, preferably behind a fence, where you grow a number of plants ready to be moved into the garden as replacements after damage has been done.

As to USDA Zones, zones can often be modified by gardeners experimenting with protected places, or in what are called *microclimates*. These are spots where temperatures are somewhat moderated by windscreens, outbuildings, or even below-ground septic tanks or sewer lines.

The soil descriptions here rely on some knowledge. Poor soil means rocky, heavy clay, surface shale, etc. Good soil can be worked without a pickax, and has a reasonable amount of humus and other soil conditioners. Excellent soil has high fertility and good drainage, and you can plunge a shovel into the ground up to the top of the blade without using a sledgehammer.

## Annuals and Biennials

Before going through this section, be warned that deer have a fondness for hollyhocks (*Alcea rosea*), all sorts of impatiens (*Impatiens* spp.), and Mexican sunflowers (*Tithonia rotundifolia*). If you want to grow these plants, provide heavy protection.

- Floss-flowers (*Ageratum houstonianum*) are tender annuals that bloom with small balls of fluffy flowers, usually in many shades of blue and pink and white, and are useful in borders or massed for color. Plants are short, usually under a foot high. Originally imported from Mexico, they are killed by the first frosts of fall.

- Forget-me-not (*Anchusa capensis*) is a biennial treated as an annual, originally from Africa and bearing flowers of forget-me-not blue (though sometimes pink or white). Best used in mass plantings, they are also very fine growing in pots.

- Snapdragons (*Antirrhinum majus*) rank at the top of the list of popular garden flowers and are especially valuable because the flowers open from the bottom up instead of the top down. Although plants will over-winter in warmer climates, for most gardeners they are annuals. Cultivars are legion, with single and double flowers blooming on stems that range from dwarf to over two feet in height. Unlike most plants that are treated as annuals, snapdragons do not like heavy clay soil, so mix in some additional compost when planting out.

- Wax begonia (*Begonia* x *semperflorens-cultorum*) are usually grown as edging plants and will bloom all summer long until cut down by frost. They adapt to

full sun but prefer some afternoon shade, especially
down south. Unless you are interested in the newest
of the new, don't bother growing these from seed, as
garden centers always have a good selection.

- Calendula (*Calendula officinalis*) are annuals of long
standing, native to the Mediterranean region, with
large flower heads up to four inches across in colors
ranging from pale yellow to deep orange. Deadhead
these plants to prolong the blooms. In times past, a
yellow dye was made from the petals to color and flavor custard dishes.

- Madagascar periwinkle (*Catharanthus roseus*) is a trailing perennial that is treated as an annual below
USDA Zone 9. This plant generates a crystalline alkaloid called vincaleukoblastine, abbreviated to VLB,
which has been found to have promise as a cancer
therapy. It's perfect for hanging baskets.

- Dusty millers (*Centaurea* spp.) comprise a number of
Mediterranean perennials that like well-drained soils
and full sun. Flowers are small and insignificant, but
the silvery gray, feathered foliage is often brushed
with powdered silver. They are excellent seaside
plants. Look for 'Silverdust'.

- Because of their tall habit, spider flowers or cleomes
(*Cleome hasslerana*) look like perennials but are really
annuals of great beauty. From a gardener's point of
view, it's wonderful that cleomes are deer resistant.
They reach six feet, and when massed in large group-

ings make a great statement, especially because they adapt to most soil conditions. The stems and leaves have a slight stickiness and there are very small thorns here and there. Colors range from white to deep violet, and many cultivars are available.

- Woodchucks (or groundhogs) love young dahlias (*Dahlia* spp.), but deer seem to dislike the taste. These are tender perennials from Mexico, grown as annuals in most gardens. The plants range from small to stately and bloom all summer with many-petalled flowers. If dug up in the fall, the tubers can be used year after year. Dahlias will grow the first year from seed, but if set out in the border, remember the smaller pests like them, especially the red-leafed varieties. Dahlias need good garden soil, plenty of water, and full sun.

- Datura or angel's trumpets (*Datura inoxia* and *D. metel*) are the annual form of a deadly family of plants infamous as the source of the drug scopolamine, a fact known to the majority of deer. The trumpet-shaped flowers are large, white or sometimes purple, and sweet smelling, but the plants themselves have an unpleasant, foxy odor. Single- and double-flowered cultivars are available. Another member of the tribe is jimson weed (*D. stramonium*), with off-white flowers and ill-smelling foliage. While beautiful, these are very dangerous plants, as all the parts are poisonous, the seeds being the worst.

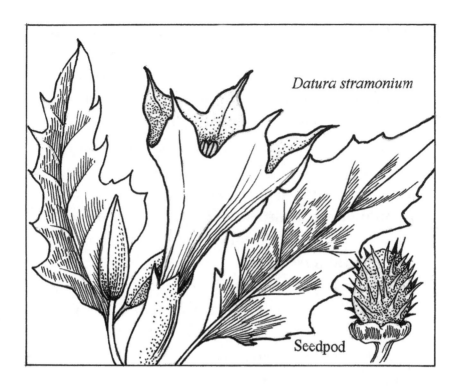

*Datura stramonium*

Seedpod

- Sweet Williams (*Dianthus barbatus*) are old-fashioned biennials that will often bloom the first year if seed is started in late winter or very early spring. As members of the pink family, they are pleasantly fragrant and great as cut flowers.
- Foxgloves (*Digitalis purpurea*) are famous biennials that bloom on three-foot-tall stems, crowded with dozens of white, pink, or cerise pouch-like flowers of great beauty. Once in your garden, they reseed with ease. These plants are the source of the heart stimulant digitalis, and apparently the drug is just as dangerous for deer as it is for humans, so they give this plant a wide berth.

- Blanket flowers (*Gaillardia pulchella*) are native annuals—named in honor of colorful Indian blankets—originally from the Southeast and Mexico. They produce daisy-like blossoms of yellow, orange, or red, with reddish bands on stems up to twenty inches high. They are great for the bed or border, tolerating a number of conditions.

- Heliotropes (*Heliotropium arborescens*) are sweet-smelling tropical perennials from Peru, usually grown as annuals. Often used for perfume, they have been popular in summer gardens for centuries. Plants up to two feet high bear myriad small, intensely fragrant flowers, usually violet or purple, though pastels and whites are available. Plants need good soil and plenty of sun.

- Polka-dot plants (*Hypoestes phyllostachya*) are tropical plants from Madagascar, long popular as houseplants not because of their small purple flowers but because of the large oval leaves liberally spotted with tiny pink dots (in cultivars, the dots are sometimes white). They do well in average but well-drained garden soil and can be dug up in the fall and moved indoors to bring color to a gray winter.

- Morning glories (*Ipomoea purpurea*) that deer resent are annual, rarely perennial, twiners that bear three-parted leaves and very showy flowers. Four inches wide or more, the flowers range from purple and white to red, blue, and pink, and are often streaked and striped. Imperial Japanese morning glories are included in this genus. They will also do well in pots and ask only for strings to climb.

- Sweet peas (*Lathyrus odoratus*) have been garden favorites in England since the first seeds landed on those shores back in 1699. The English have doted on them ever since. Why deer usually leave them alone is not understood, but a number of gardeners told me that is the case. Sweet peas need deep, moist, cool, and well-prepared soil and should be started in the garden as soon as the soil can be worked. They do not do well in very warm climates.

- Limoniums (*Limonium* spp.) are a large family of plants, also called sea lavenders, with two-foot stems bearing clusters of tiny flowers surrounded with bright, papery wraps. They are fine in bouquets and in dried arrangements. Three species are usually sold—often interchanged—and usually sold as annuals, so it's best just to look for statice. Colors run the spectrum, with red and orange very popular.

- Flax (*Linum usitatissimum*) originally came from Asia and has survived in much of North America. Early settlers and the textile industry used the plant as a source of fibers for cloth, as well as a seed crop for the manufacture of linseed oil. Plants contain a cyanide-like compound and the oil is thought to be a purgative.

- Edging lobelias (*Lobelia erinus*) are one of the most popular plants for edgings, groundcovers, planters, and window boxes. Their cheery little blue flowers bloom all summer long and feature a number of attractive cultivars. The plants contain a poisonous alkaloid called lobelic acid that should not be eaten. Obviously deer know all about it, too.

- Four o'clock (*Mirabilis jalapa*), or in older books, the miracle of Peru, are tender, tropical perennials that bloom the first year from seed. The three- to four-foot plants sport nocturnal, sweet-smelling flowers of attractive colors including red, pink, white, crimson, and yellow. The plants spring from potato-sized black tubers that can be dug up in the fall and stored over winter in a cool, dry place. Four o'clock roots are the source of a fast-acting purgative drug known as jalap, which might explain deer's aversion to this plant.

- Opium poppies (*Papaver somniferum*) are the source of opium and, except for the seeds, full of toxic alkaloids. The production of opium is, of course, illegal in the United States; it's also illegal to grow these flowers, so the nursery industry now calls them "peony-flowered poppies" and ducks the issue. Plants can grow to five feet and bear blossoms up to five inches wide. There are all sorts of cultivars leading to many single and double blossoms of great color combinations. And by planting seeds every few weeks over the summer, flowers will bloom until frost cuts them down.

- Zonal geraniums (*Pelargonium* x *hortorum*) are very popular summer bedding plants with large, usually red, blossoms on stout stems. The plants have various zones of color on the leaves and a very strong scent. They like hot weather and plenty of sun, and should be deadheaded as the flowers fade.

- Petunias (*Petunia* x *hybrida*) are closely related to tobacco and, as such, have moderately sticky stems and a bitter taste. They are one of the most popular bedding annuals for gardens across the country. Flowers come in many colors, including striped, and look great in baskets or in a border. Again, the selection of plants at garden centers precludes starting them from seed.

- Castor beans (*Ricinus communis*) are among the most poisonous of plants. These are fast-growing annuals with huge, cut leaves with up to eleven lobes in dark purple, deep green, or a bronzed green. Small flowers turn into prickly fruits that contain the shiny beans. These tropical-looking beauties come in many cultivars and are still available from the more adventurous seed companies. All parts of the plant are poisonous. Frequently, American nurseries have dropped castor beans from their catalogs, due to worries about lawsuits. But they are easily obtained from seed houses in Canada and England.

- Blue salvia (*Salvia farinacea*) is a tender perennial native to Texas and New Mexico, not reliably hardy in most of the U.S. and thus treated as an annual. The violet-blue flowers are an inch long and grow in spikes up to three feet high. The calyx, the cupped part of the flower that holds the petals, is dusted with a white powder, hence the other common name: mealycup sage. I suspect deer dislike the powder. Provide good garden soil and plenty of sun.

- St. Mary's thistle (*Silybum marianum*) is a member of the thistle family, having basal leaves up to fourteen inches long and very lobed and spiny. The surface is decorated with a fine network of veins and spots of silvery white. Toward late summer, light-purple thistle-like flowers, about two inches across, appear on tall stems. These plants can subsist on poor and dry soil.

- Marigolds (*Tagetes* spp.) are strong-smelling annuals, well known in the nursery trade as one of the most popular of summer bedding plants. Today there are hundreds of cultivars, usually in shades of yellow, orange, tan, and almost white. They are great in beds or borders, for edging, in containers or baskets, and even in the vegetable garden, as the roots produce a chemical that repels nematodes.

- Verbena (*Verbena* x *hybrida*) is a perennial hybrid that freely blooms from seed the first year. The flowers are attractive and bloom in a number of colors, looking especially pretty when massed together. Provide good garden soil and plenty of sun.

## Herbs, Vegetables, and Fruits

The following, smaller list includes herbs and vegetables—in general, plants known for flavor, texture, or both. (Though I didn't include it below, Patrik Battle, a fellow organic gardener in Asheville, advised me that deer also do not disturb turnips.)

- The onion species (*Allium* spp.) in general is passed over by deer. Chives (*Allium schoenoporasum*) perform two duties in the garden: They bear attractive flowers most of the summer, and the hollow leaves, when cut into small sections, give an incredible zest to cottage cheese. Garlic chives (*A. tuberosum*) bear leaves with more of a garlicky flavor and the white flowers are great sprinkled on a salad.

- Angelicas (*Angelica archangelica*), also known as wild parsnips, are biennials, blooming the second year. They prefer a cool, moist spot in the garden and produce grapefruit-sized umbels of attractive, yellow-green flowers in early summer. The stems are candied and the plant is also used to flavor liqueurs.

- Wormwoods (*Artemisia absinthium*) are extremely bitter perennial herbs, native to Europe but now naturalized in the Northeast. All parts of the plant have an unforgettable flavor. Wormwood prefers dry soil and full sun, the silvery leaves are very attractive, and small yellow flowers appear in late summer. The liquor absinthe is made from wormwood—illegal because it's habit-forming and leads to delirium, hallucinations, and permanent mental decline. No wonder deer leave wormwood alone! Russian tarragon (*A. dranunculus*) is an herbaceous perennial, with two-foot stems and aromatic leaves, often found in kitchen gardens.

- The papaw (*Asimina triloba*) is a deciduous shrub that can, in the wild, reach a thirty-foot height. It bears a five-inch edible fruit beloved by some, but luckily for landscaping, deer usually ignore the plant.

- Borage (*Borago officinalis*) is an annual that looks like a perennial, having drooping sprays of attractive flowers and delicate hairs covering the entire plant. Young leaves have a cucumber-like fragrance and are great when added to summer drinks, ciders, and wines. Try freezing borage flowers in ice cubes for a great garnish.

- Caraway (*Carum carvi*) is an erect biennial with an overwintering taproot. The seeds are used to flavor breads, meats, and cheeses, and are the basis for the liqueur kümmel—a drink you might use to salute your success (or failure) in fighting deer.

- Basket flowers (*Centaurea americana*) bear a single flower, with a base resembling a woven basket, on a three- to four-foot stem. The blossoms close at night. Bachelor's button (*C. cyanus*), or cornflower, is a familiar annual that flowers in white, pink, rose, purple, red, and blue.

- Pyrethrum (*Chrysanthemum parthenium*) is a perennial member of the great mum family, native to Yugoslavia, and the source of the pyrethrum used to fight a number of insects. Prolonged contact with the plant can cause skin irritations and other possible allergies in humans. With long, gray, finely divided leaves and clusters of small, white, daisy-like flowers, pyrethrum looks great in the border.

- Lots of people love the pungent flavor of coriander or Chinese parsley (*Coriandrum sativum*), but deer seem to disagree. Small, pinkish-white flowers bloom in composite umbels, followed by round, yellow-brown seeds in May and June. The seeds smell of lemon or orange peel with an overlay of sage. It's a staple in Indian cuisine.

- Cosmos daisies (*Cosmos bipinnatus*) bloom all summer long, with attractive daisy-like blossoms in white or pink, and are mainstays of any garden. Even the fern-like foliage is attractive. These are great plants for a cutting garden.

- Globe artichoke and cardoons (*Cynara scolymus*) are very large border plants with heavily cut, silvery foliage of great beauty. Artichokes are grown for their fruit and cardoons for flowers and general habit (although Italian cooks often cut the stems in sections and deep-fry them). With protection, they stay hardy to USDA Zone 6.

- Persimmons (*Diospyros virginiana*) are large shrubs or small trees grown for their interesting foliage and picturesque habit, not to mention their edible fruits. With sun, good drainage, and a decent soil, they can withstand city conditions. Persimmons are difficult to transplant, so buy them potted or as a professionally balled-and-burlaped tree.

- The golden flowers of California poppies (*Eschsholzia californica*) once were so thick along the coastline that early explorers shouted, "Gold! Gold!" when they first saw the blooms. Perennials in warmer climates, they are treated as annuals in most of the country.
- While not reliably hardy throughout the United States, the edible fig (*Ficus carica*) is easily grown in a pot below USDA Zones 8 and 9. The cultivars 'Brown Turkey' and 'Celeste' are hardy to Zone 7 and are self-pollinating, a necessity with figs. In Zone 6, gardeners often bend the soft trunks slowly to the ground, then cover the plants and mulch well. They usually survive.
- Fennel (*Foeniculum vulgare*) is a favorite herb, used for flavorings and as a hot tea to relieve tension (including nervous problems resulting from deer rampages). The plants are food for swallowtail caterpillars and should be grown for that reason alone. Leaves contribute an anise flavor to foods and salads.
- Sweet woodruff (*Galium odoratum*) is a perennial that lives in the woodlands of central Europe. A creeping rhizome sends up erect stems about ten inches high, with whorls of dark green leaves and clusters of small, white, star-like flowers. The leaves contain courmarin, a chemical that smells like new-mown hay or vanilla. Courmarin is a blood thinner and is actually

used in the rat poison known as Warfarin. Perhaps the deer know something?

- Jerusalem artichokes (*Helianthus tuberosus*) are tall members of the sunflower clan with twelve-foot stems and edible, potato-like tubers especially good for diabetics. They were an important food for Native Americans.

- Walnuts (*Juglens nigra*) are stately native trees known for their ability to kill other plants grown in their vicinity—the roots produce a chemical called juglens. That said, they are great shade trees—initially they grow quickly, and at a certain height are usually left alone. Younger trees should be planted in tree tubes to prevent deer browsing.

- English lavender (*Lavandula angustifolia*) is a beloved herb with that special scent that's been used in toiletries since the Middle Ages. The entire plant is covered with short, wooly hairs, and in early summer, tall spikes topped with lavender to purple flowers appear and attract bees and butterflies. Spanish or French lavender (*L. stoechas*) also does well in a hot, dry spot in the garden but is not as hardy as the English variety.

- Mint (*Mentha* spp.) is represented by a number of perennial plants that adapt to poor soil and damp conditions by spreading far and wide using both surface and underground runners. It can be a pest, but deer dislike mint, giving it an edge in the herb garden. Because it grows with such vigor, mint has a ten-

dency to exhaust the soil over a few years' time, so
crop rotation is a necessity.

- Bee balm or Oswego tea (*Monarda didyma*) is a stout,
very upright, aromatic perennial to four feet, native
to the East Coast (and inland), bearing red, tubular
flowers that bloom in dense whorls and are beloved
by hummingbirds and nectar-seeking insects. It was
first observed by the English in 1637 and was a hit in
European gardens right from the beginning. It likes
a good, moist soil and partial shade. Mature clumps
should be divided. An oil from this plant is used to
hide unpleasant-smelling chemicals.

- Sweet cicely (*Myrrhis odorata*) is a graceful perennial
that grows to a height of about three feet. The fern-
like leaves have a strong scent of anise. Small,
creamy-white flowers bloom in large umbels in late
spring to early summer. The ripening seedpods are
an inch long and shiny black. Early settlers brought
this plant from Europe, using the stalks as flavorings
and sweeteners for conserves.

- Catnips (*Nepeta cataria*) are branched perennials
about three feet high, originally from Eurasia. The
stems and leaves have a soft, gray, hairy down, giving
catnip the look of being dusted with hoarfrost. In
summer, small purple and white flowers bloom in
dense whorls and from a distance look like a blue
mist. Provide a good soil and sunlight. Catmint (*N.
mussinii*) flops over and is only about a foot high and

has bluer flowers. The odor of catnip is addictive to most cats, and perhaps deer dislike the association.

- Sweet basil (*Ocimum basilicum*) is a marvelously flavored herb found in every good garden. It's used for both flavor and for the decorative leaves.

- Prickly pears (*Opuntia* spp.) have too many hair-like spines for deer to bother with eating the padded stems. These natives produce a profusion of beautiful yellow flowers in late spring to early summer. The seedpods are very good when prepared in Tex-Mex dishes.

- Marjoram (*Origanum* spp.) is a common name for a number of garden herbs that belong to the mint family and are grown for flavoring foods. They want full sun. Common oregano (*O. vulgare*) is especially useful as a groundcover and the cultivar 'Aureum' has leaves of golden green.

- Parsley (*Petroselinum crispum*) is grown in most gardens as a garnish for all sorts of foods but can also be utilized as a great edging plant. Plant several sowings to guarantee a continual supply for summer meals.

- Rhubarb (*Rheum rhabarbarum*) is usually grown for its tall stalks, which are cooked in various ways and often mixed with fruits such as strawberries. It provides a noble aspect and is often used as a perennial. The leaves contain a toxic chemical (anthraquinone glycosides) and deer give it a wide berth. Rhubarb does not grow well in very hot climates.

- Rosemary (*Rosmarinus officinalis*) is a beautiful herbal treat from around the Mediterranean Sea. Being quite piquant in flavor, it is disliked by deer. For gardeners in USDA Zone 6, there is a cultivar called 'Salem' that is fairly resistant to winter chills—as long as it gets perfect drainage.

- Black-eyed Susans (*Rudbeckia* spp.) were well known in wildflower gardens back in the 1800s and were favorites of Thoreau. Classified as an annual, biennial, or short-lived perennial, these great wildflowers have bristly-hairy leaves, making them a problem for highly allergic gardeners. The flower disks are bright yellow surrounded by drooping ray flowers. Native Americans used the roots to treat many illnesses. They do well in poor but well-drained soil. There are reports of deer sometimes eating these plants, but they have to be very hungry to do so.

- Sage (*Salvia officinalis*) is a very aromatic herb native to the Mediterranean region. Cultivars provide various leaf colors, with 'Tricolor' being especially attractive in the garden.

- Perennial soapwort (*Saponaria officinalis*) contains a frothing chemical called saponin that dissolves grease. Because of its gentle action, soapwort continues to be used for cleaning precious linens such as tapestries and canvases. The pink, tubular flowers are very attractive, scented by night, and bloom for a long period in early summer. This is an unfussy plant

that will survive in the garden for decades if left
undisturbed.

- Potatoes (*Solanum tuberosum*) probably would be
  loved by deer if they found them suitably prepared
  for their table, but being members of the vastly poisonous tomato family, plants are shunned by deer.
- Spanish broom or weaver's broom (*Spartium
  junceum*) is a small shrub from the south of Europe
  used as an ornamental. There's only one species in
  the genus, which is related to the dyer's broom
  (*Genista* spp.) but has larger flowers. The fragrant,
  one-inch-long blooms are a bright yellow and look
  like the typical pea flower. The flower is followed by a
  small, thin peapod. Leaves are few and simple in
  shape. At home in dry soil, this is an ideal plant for a
  xeriscape garden, and as such is fairly common in
  California. A very strong fiber is obtained from this
  plant and used in the manufacture of rope. It also
  has some medicinal uses and was once used as a
  purgative, emetic, and diuretic. It likes full sun, and
  well-drained and slightly alkaline soil, and is hardy to
  USDA Zone 7. This one is worth growing in pots and
  keeping in a warm place where winters are severe.
  Prune to the ground if it gets scraggly.
- Lamb's ears (*Stachys byzantina*) are named in refer-
  ence to their silver-gray, felty leaves. Pink to lavender
  flowers are borne in whorls on leaved stalks up to
  eighteen inches high. They are great garden plants
  but dislike heavy clay soil and extended wet winters.

In the Middle Ages, the leaves were used to bandage wounds.

- Blueberries (*Vaccinium* spp.) are not only good to eat but they are an attractive shrub, up to eight feet tall, with pleasant flowers and great fruit. They do well in acid soil. The rabbiteye blueberry (*V. ashei*) reaches a height of four to six feet with a five-foot spread and glossy, green foliage, turning a dull red in the fall, and bearing sky-blue berries. These are great plants for a hedge or a border—but remember, while deer ignore blueberries, birds love them. My Sullivan County friend, Ben Wechsler, reminded me that he once noticed deer nosing around a big patch of blueberries, and upon investigation he found that, in the shade of the shrubs, some blackberry vines were growing and the deer were eating the blackberry leaves.

## Perennials for the Garden and the Border

Before growing the following plants, again be warned that deer have a fondness for daylilies (*Hemerocallis* spp.), hostas (*Hosta* spp.), cardinal flowers (*Lobelia cardinalis*), all sorts of phloxes (*Phlox* spp.), and roses (*Rosa* spp.) of almost any variety—and that includes those with thorns. Deer are able to purse their lips in order to avoid thorn damage. They will also sometimes eat wild geraniums or cranebills (*Geranium maculatum*).

Here's the major list for gardeners. These plants have a history of generally (note the word *generally*) being left alone by most deer. This does not mean that deer haven't attacked some of these plants in the past or might decide to do so in the future. But for all practical purposes, deer leave the following plants alone. Whenever possible, I've given the reason for their dislikes.

- Yarrows (*Achillea* spp.) are attractive plants grown in the garden proper, the rock garden, and the herb garden. They prefer a lot of sun, and the common yarrow (*A. millefolium*) has produced a number of attractive cultivars with tightly bunched flower heads of unusual colors.

- The monkshood (*Aconitum* spp.) bears unusual-looking flowers, prefers partial shade, and is very attractive planted in groups. The roots and most of the plant are poisonous to most mammals (and are often used as a murder weapon in detective novels). Provide moist soil and partial shade. You might have to stake the taller varieties.

- Bishop's weed (*Aegopodium podagraria*) is one of the most despised weeds of England, known there as ground elder. Here's a plant that the whole of Great Britain wishes were a deer favorite, but it isn't. While the species is somewhat attractive, its exuberant habits outweigh its usefulness. But for an attractive groundcover with reasonably nice flowers, try the variegated form 'Variegatum,' with leaves margined in white.

- The century plant (*Agave americana*) does not require a hundred years to bloom (more like thirty-five), but it's a great perennial for a desert garden or in pots

where the climate is cold. They need full sun and
well-drained soil.

- Carpet bugle weeds (*Ajuga reptans*) are attractive and
tough groundcovers with pretty spring flowers resembling tiny snapdragons. There are many cultivars producing leaves with variegations or unusual shades of
green. These plants have a tendency to invade
lawns—a fact that I, who do not spend hours with a
lawn, rather enjoy.

- Amsonias (*Amsonia tabernaemontana*) are clump-form-
ing, native perennials with three-foot stems topped
with powder-blue flowers. They bloom from spring
into early summer, and longer if deadheaded. The
sap is milky and, I suspect, quite bitter. In the North,
grow them as annuals.

- Pearly everlastings (*Anaphalis margaritacea*) were often found in farmhouse bouquets, as the flowers
have strawlike petals and last virtually forever. Native
Americans used them to treat diarrhea, dysentery,
and bronchial coughs. They do well in poor but well-
drained soil in full sun.

- Anemones or windflowers (*Anemone* spp.) belong to
the buttercup family and produce beautiful, petalled
flowers. The florist's anemone (*A. coronaria*) can be
grown in pots, the beautiful Pasque flower (*A. patens*)
for rock gardens in the spring, and the majority, including the Japanese anemone (*A.* x *hybrida*) for
great autumn bloom. They need a good garden soil
and partial shade.

- Columbines (*Aquilegia* spp.) are beautiful, native American wildflowers, and are also represented by some great garden perennials originally sired in Europe. The smaller types are perfect for the rock garden and the larger for the border. They benefit from deadheading. Although seeds of the wild columbine (*A. canadensis*) were used by the Native Americans as a cure for headaches, they are potentially poisonous.

- Jack-in-the-pulpit (*Arisaema triphyllum*) are woodland flowers of great interest thanks to the flowers, which consist of a fleshy green to purple spadex (or Jack), enclosed by a hooded and striped spathe (or pulpit). The dried corms were used medicinally by Native Americans and, when boiled a number of times, make a palatable food. Corms and other plant parts are rich in crystals of calcium oxalate and are known to cause intense irritation and burning in the mouth.

- Giant reed grass (*Arundo donax*) can reach a height of eighteen feet, putting it out of reach of most deer. It is also very invasive, eventually producing vast groves of bamboo-like stems (or culms). The variety 'Variegata' has attractive blades with white stripes and is not as invasive as the parent species. The dried culms are used to make clarinet reeds.

- Goatsbeard (*Aruncus dioicus*) is a native plant edged with graceful leaves and crowned with pyramidal plumes of tiny white flowers. It makes an excellent plant for the wildflower or proper garden. The roots were once pounded into poultices to treat bee stings and for a root tea used to ease bleeding after child-birth.

- Butterfly weed (*Asclepias tuberosa*) is a native plant of great beauty that should be in all American gardens. The plants are drought-resistant and the usually long-lasting, orange flowers, blooming in early summer, are especially attractive to butterflies. They do not transplant well, so buy plants in pots or grow them from seed. There are a number of attractive cultivars. The spent flowers eventually form seedpods with silvery tufts of hair that fly in the wind.

- Originally from Southern Europe and Turkey, basket-of-gold (*Aurinia saxatilis*) is a favorite for early spring rock gardens because of its long panicles of pale yellow against a background of silvery gray leaves. There are many cultivars in various shades of yellow, and the plants adapt to growing in walls with ease. Well-drained soil and full sun are preferred.

- Astilbe (*Astilbe* spp.) are garden favorites because of their attractive and deeply cut foliage and tall, spire-like branches of tiny flowers. They are easy to grow but need good garden soil and plenty of moisture at the roots. Here's a perfect plant for waterside plantings. There are a number of cultivars with exceptional colors on today's market.

- False indigo (*Baptisia* spp.) is an American native, growing as a three- to six-foot, bush-like plant, almost a deciduous shrub, and is really a thing of beauty in the garden. Strong stems bear blue-green, oblong leaves and pea-like indigo flowers in late spring. The spent flowers give way to inflated, brown pea pods that rattle with the enclosed seeds and were once used as children's toys. The entire plant turns black when hit by frost. Once settled in, this is a very drought-resistant plant. *B. alba* is a beautiful species with heavy clusters of white flowers.

- The winter begonias (*Bergenia cordifolia*) bear clump-growing, stout, cabbage-like leaves that, with time, can form large colonies. Nodding, bell-like flowers appear in early spring or late winter, and south of USDA Zone 7, the leaves are usually evergreen. *B.* x *schmidtii* is the hybrid usually sold in nurseries. In the South they must have partial shade.

- Cross vines (*Bignonia capreolata*) are evergreen climbers that ramble over stone walls, fences, and random rocks. The common name refers to the cross made visible when you cut a cross-section of a stem. In winter, leaves turn a deep burgundy, and in late spring the vines burst forth with orange, trumpet-shaped flowers. While somewhat aggressive, it can be controlled. Provide full sun.

- Boltonias (*Boltonia asteroids*) are white-flowered wild-flower members of the aster family, sometimes reaching a six-foot height and covered with starry blossoms in late summer and early fall. When sited in a good spot, they eventually form a large group of plants.

- Heathers (*Calluna vulgaris*) comprise one species of usually low-growing evergreen shrubs, originally from

Europe and the hills of Scotland. An amazing number of cultivars have been developed, with many colors to the small, numerous flowers. Colors range from white to pink to red and beyond. Since the Scots have almost as much trouble with deer as Americans, it's lucky that our hoofed friends generally ignore heathers. Heathers prefer very acid soil and excellent drainage.

- The bellflower (*Campanula glomerata*) is a rather coarse, erect perennial to three feet bearing bell-like flowers of blue or white, having arrived on our shores from Eurasia. There are a few cultivars available. Canterbury bells (*C. medium*) arrived from Europe and are biennials to three feet high—while seemingly ignored by deer, they have been nibbled by woodchucks along one of our garden paths. The mountain harebell (*C. rotundifolia*) has flowers of white to a deep lavender blue.

- Bluebeards (*Caryopteris* x *clandonensis*) are not reliably hardy below USDA Zone 7, but where the weather is warm enough, they grow as low shrubs on stout stems and bear attractive flowers of blue, lavender, or white.

- Bittersweet (*Celastrus* spp.) is a vine that is not only a killer of other trees and shrubs but one of the most invasive plants east of the Mississippi. There are two garden species, the American bittersweet (*C. scandens*), its gene pool now mostly corrupted by the invader, the oriental bittersweet (*C. orbiculatus*).

*Celastrus orbiculatus*

Sadly, this invader, which can take over just about all in its path, is ignored by deer. If you do grow this plant—its berries dot the fall landscape with the brightest of oranges and reds—make sure you do not let it seed about in your yard.

- Knapweeds (*Centaurea* spp.) are a large family of plants (between 400 and 500 species of annuals, biennials, and perennials). In the perennial class, there is one particular species known as *C. macrocephala*, an erect plant to about three feet bearing golden yellow flowers of great charm, loved by bees, and described in botanical terms as being scabrous or rough to the touch, with many small, annoying projections. Provide average garden soil and full sun.

- Snow-in-summer (*Cerastium tomentosum*) grows as a mat-forming perennial in well-drained soil and full sun. They have white, wooly, one-inch leaves on trailing stems and bear one-inch-wide showy white flowers. Deer dislike the wooly part.

- Shasta daisies (*Chrysanthemum* x *superbum*) were created by America's most famous botanist and plant breeder, Luther Burbank. They bear large, daisy-like blossoms on top of three-foot stems and make great cutting flowers.

- The bugbanes (*Cimicifuga* spp.) are native American plants of great beauty, having very attractive foliage, doing well in partial shade, and bearing tall spires of tiny, white, petal-less flowers that resemble white candles. There are many species available, but my favorite is the summer cohosh (*C. Americana*), usually topping out at six feet. Provide a good moist soil and, of course, partial shade. That this plant is deer-resistant is a blessing for gardeners.

- For years I grew the wild clematis, old-man's beard, or virgin's bower (*Clematis virginiana*), not for the small white flowers but for the great silver-toned, feathery seedpods that appear in late summer to early fall. Clematises like a cool root run, with the rest of the vine in good light to full sun. They clamber through branches without any harm to the host plant or tree. To see the seedpods glistening on the autumn vines alone is worth the price of admission.

- Turtleheads (*Cleone glabra*) are aptly named perennials with blossoms that closely resemble a turtle's (or perhaps a lizard's) head. The bunches of flowers bloom on top of a two- to three-foot stem and were used by early settlers to make an ointment to treat piles, painful ulcers, and herpes. Turtleheads prefer partial shade and damp to moist soil, doing well when planted at the edge of a stream or small pond.

- Lily-of-the-valley (*Convallaria majalis*) is the beloved, sweetly fragrant species bearing drooping, bell-shaped flowers with cut edges in mid-spring. Originally from Europe, they have naturalized in the U.S., having been brought over by the colonists as a reminder of home. The early settlers used a tea concocted from the roots to treat heart disease and as a substitute for digitalis (see foxglove). Over many years of walking the Appalachian Trail above Hot Springs, North Carolina, I noticed that although deer abound, the lily-of-the-valley never seem to be bothered, so I assume, especially from their use as medicines, that the taste must not be pleasant.

- The perennial coreopsis (*Coreopsis grandiflora*) reaches a two-foot height and bears yellow to orange blooms. Native to the Midwest and as far south as Florida, it needs full sun.

- Pampas grass (*Cortaderia selloana*) is one of those ornamental grasses that became a cliché before its time. When driving in most of South Carolina and northern Florida, you'll see this grass alongside driveways to homes, farms, and motels. They are rarely damaged by deer, so every fall their plume-like blossoms stand tall on eight-foot stems, resembling the fans that Cleopatra's slaves used to cool her royal forehead. Provide well-drained soil and full sun.

- Turkey corn or wild bleeding heart (*Dicentra exima*) are native perennial wildflowers usually grown in the wildflower garden for their interesting flowers. They need a good, fertile soil in light shade.

- Few gardeners know what a great perennial the gas plant (*Dictamnus albus*) can be. The common name comes from the fact that gas plant seedpods, when squeezed, will produce a whiff of flammable liquid that burns for a moment with a blue flame. They have a distinctive, heavy citrus smell that deer apparently dislike. Never transplant gas plants, as they resent any disturbance to the roots. For the garden, buy one in a pot.

- Over the past ten years, purple coneflowers (*Echinacea purpurea*) have achieved almost cult status for gardeners. These daisy-like flowers have a sharp and prickly central cone surrounded by weeping pink petals (really ray flowers), on strong, two- to three-foot stems. They are especially valuable in the drug industry—and that, plus the prickly flowers, could explain deer's reluctance to eat these blossoms. Provide a good soil and full sun.

- Globe thistles (*Echinops* spp.) are tall plants with interesting and beautiful cut leaves and round blossoms made up of many individual flowers, mostly of striking metallic blue. They are not fussy as to soil but do like plenty of sunlight. In most of the species, the leaves have spiny-toothed margins.
- Viper's bugloss (*Echium fastuosum*) hails from the Canary Islands, where it produces purple panicles or dark blue flowers on six-foot, scabrous stems. They are greenhouse or pot plants outside the warmer parts of the country, as they succumb to freezing. That said, they are beautiful in the garden.
- Barrenwort (*Epimedium* spp.) are great groundcovers that bear attractive compound leaves on wiry stems and, in spring, flowers that resemble a bishop's mitered cap. There are a number of species, and in general deer choose to ignore them. They do well in average garden soil with partial shade.
- Horsetail or scouring rush (*Equisetum hyemale*) is a perennial plant closely related to the ferns; its giant ancestors grew twenty feet tall and formed much of what makes up today's coal deposits. They are adaptable plants and, as such, great runners, and so are best when contained. From deeply buried rhizomes grow erect, green, ribbed, hollow-jointed stems resembling children's beads known as "pop-its." Plant them at the edge of a pond or in pots set directly in a

pool or on the terrace. The silica-heavy stems were once used to scour greasy pots and pans.

- Heaths (*Erica* spp.) are generally thought of as being companions to heathers, except there are more than one species available. They are rock garden and alpine plants that flower, according to type, throughout the year but are best kept for the winter garden. They need acid soil and perfect drainage to succeed.

- Joe-Pye weed (*Eupatorium* spp.) was named for a white man who posed as a native medicine man in order to sell a folk remedy for the cure of scarlet fever, made from the roots of this plant. In moist soil and full sun, plants often top fourteen feet with beautiful plumes of light lavender flowers at the top. They are beloved by butterflies. Another member of this genus is the snakeroot (*E. rugosum*), a handsome, fall-blooming plant with small, fuzzy, white flowerheads entirely made of disk flowers. It loves a woodsy setting and is a great addition to the fall garden. When eaten by cows, this plant can poison their milk, in some cases leading to fatalities (Abraham Lincoln's mother died from drinking such milk).

- Queen-of-the-prairie (*Filipendula* spp.) is a handsome member of the rose family that blooms with pinkish-red blossoms in terminal clusters that look for all the world like cotton candy. This plant has a high tannin content (tannin was once used to cure leather) and astringent properties. It also contains a chemical forerunner of aspirin known as salicin. Provide good garden soil and good drainage.

- Creeping wintergreen or teaberry (*Gaultheria procumbens*) is a popular wildflower of a crawling habit. This low-growing, evergreen shrub of small stature bears white, nodding, bell-shaped flowers that mature as edible, bright red, pulpy, berry-like capsules. The leaves have a distinct wintergreen flavor. Extract of teaberry is used to spice many products, including chewing gum.

- Carolina jessamine (*Gelsemum sempervirens*) is an American native often seen growing up trees and over and under fences in the Southeast—hence it serves as a great screening material. The vine reaches a length of about twenty feet, with attractive pointed leaves and fragrant, yellow, tubular flowers blooming singly or in small bunches. Tolerant as to soil but demanding as much sun as possible, this is a great plant for the home garden. There is a double-flowered cultivar, 'Pride of Augusta'. Jessamines are hardy from USDA Zones 6 to 9.

- Avens (*Geum* spp.) are great perennials with many species popular in gardens. One particular species, *G. quellyon*, has produced a number of very colorful cultivars, including the famous 'Mrs. Bradshaw' with red flowers and 'Lady Stratheden' with yellow flowers. The stems and the leaves are hairy. Water avens (*G. rivale*) bears dull, reddish, nodding flowers, and grows in bogs, water gardens, and moist soil. The roots are astringent, having been used at one time as diuretics and to make a wash for skin diseases and boils.

- Baby's breath (*Gypsophila paniculata*) is often used in floral arrangements because of the airy profusion of tiny blossoms numbering in the hundreds on one stem. There are a number of cultivars available, in various colors and some with a double number of petals.

- English ivy (*Hedera helix*) is such a prolific spreader that, even if some of your output is eaten by deer, in the end you'll probably applaud their efforts. Once established, ivy can take over everything within its reach. Some references claim that deer eat this plant with abandon, while others suggest growing it. In my experience, I've found that deer only eat this plant when nothing else is available.

- Iris (*Iris* spp.) have never been touched by deer in any of my northern gardens, but then I had so many other succulent things around that most deer would just ignore them. That said, old-fashioned flags (*I. germanica*) and the majority of bearded irises seem to escape the curse. Also, in my many woods-wanderings, I've never seen our native American wildflower, the dwarf crested iris (*I. cristata*), ever nibbled at.

- Lenten roses (*Helleborus orientalis*) bloom in late winter and early spring, producing flowers of great charm. Hellebore flowers last up to six weeks in the garden before turning to seedpods, because what look like petals are really long-lasting sepals. They have very attractive palmate leaves with serrated edges and not only provide blossoms but evergreen groundcover. The plants are also very poisonous. For gardeners who wish to live dangerously, the American white or false hellebore (*Veratrum viride*) is a perennial with pleated leaves up to six feet high, and small, star-like flowers opening as a yellow-brown but quickly turning green. Early settlers used it as a painkiller, but all parts, especially the roots, are highly toxic and ignored by deer.

- A bitter substance derived from glandular hairs on hops (*Humulus lupulus*) is used to give aroma and flavor to beer. Disorders ranging from cramps to coughs to cancer are said to be treated by chemicals from this plant, not to mention jaundice, neuralgia, and worms. The plant and all its parts are bitter. It's also a very fast growing vine and quite useful when used as a living garden screen. The pollen can cause contact dermatitis. There is a very attractive, yellow-leafed form called 'Aureus'.

- Why Japanese temple bells (*Kirengeshoma palmata*) are usually ignored by deer is anybody's guess, because these very, very attractive plants should be in every garden. The yellow, wax-like flowers bloom in early summer atop two- to three-foot-high stems, their palmate leaves deeply cut and resembling large maple leaves. They need a good, moist garden soil in partial shade.

*Iberis sempervirens*

- Loosestrife (*Lythrum salicaria*) is a plague on all our houses. The plant was brought to America for a special garden in Central Park, Manhattan, that was going to display all the flowers of Shakespeare. Now it's a major invader in both the Northeast and the Southeast—wherever there are bogs and wet meadows, loosestrife simply takes over. Garden cultivars are sterile and cause no problems; only the pure species is a problem. And wouldn't you know it? Deer dislike the plant.

- Candytuft (*Iberis sempervirens*) is known as a flowering subshrub and is a favorite in rock gardens. Plants bloom in early spring with terminal clusters of small, white flowers. The small leaves are usually evergreen except in cold climates.

- Spotted dead nettles (*Lamium maculatum*) sport oval leaves often spotted with whitish blotches, and bloom with small, snapdragon-like flowers of pink, purple, purplish-brown, and sometimes white. They adapt to most any garden conditions and have a tendency to spread about.

- Rough blazing star (*Liatris aspera*) and prairie gayfeather (*L. spicata*) are both disliked by deer. The first plant bears tall stalks, with about thirty rose-purple flowers per stalk, blooming in early summer and accustomed to dry but well-drained soil. The second is much the same, only a bit shorter. A root tea was used as a folk remedy for bladder and kidney ailments as well as some sexually transmitted diseases.

- Blue toadflax (*Linaria canadensis*) bears small, light blue-violet, spurred flowers like mini-snapdragons on plants about two feet high. They grow in open, dry, rocky sites, blooming in summer. Butter-and-eggs (*L. vulgaris*) have yellow, two-lipped, spurred flowers with an orange ridge. They grow along the roadside throughout the East, and if they weren't so common, everybody would want them.

- Perennial blue flax (*Linum perenne*) grows about two feet high, bearing pretty flowers of chicory-blue. It is related to common flax, the source of flax and of linseed oil.

- Honeysuckles (*Lonicera* spp.) are fond favorites of the garden, and our native species make great additions to the backyard. The Japanese *L. japonica* is the infamous thugee. With many varieties to choose from—some evergreen, some semi-evergreen, and a few deciduous—plus a large selection of color, there's a species right for your garden. And deer almost never eat it! When they do (and occasionally they will), you're dealing with a plant that responds with the fervor of a *Star Wars* devotee presented with a new chapter.

- Miscanthus grasses (*Miscanthus* spp.) represent a number of ornamental grasses great for the garden, not only because of their attractive leaves that grow in clumps and resemble fountains, but also for the plumelike flowers of autumn. 'Gracillimus' has a graceful form while 'Zebrinus' has leaves striped with creamy white. There are many cultivars, and all seem to be too tough for deer to enjoy the nibbling.

- Myrtle or periwinkle (*Myrtus communis*) is a creeping evergreen groundcover of great beauty that originally came over from Europe with the original settlers. Five-petalled, blue flowers appear in spring and again in fall. Although a beautiful plant, myrtle is an aggressive spreader and can easily take over a large area, choking out other plants.

- Evening primroses (*Oenothera* spp.) represent a large family of native American plants, principally the sundrops blooming by day and the evening primroses blooming by night. Sundrops stand about three feet high, are rampant spreaders, and bloom with bright yellow, four-petalled, cheery flowers that close at night. Evening primroses have the same kind of flowers but open slowly at twilight. Evening primrose oil is a natural source of gamma-linolenic acid, and the plants have been used for many medicinal purposes.

- Prickly pears (*Opuntia* spp.) bring to mind the cactus family in general. Most gardeners ignore these fascinating and drought-resistant plants because of the spines. For the same reasons, most deer avoid them, too, especially those with tiny, hair-like thorns that get into the skin (or nose) and are difficult to remove. In spite of their threatening appearance, they have downright beautiful blossoms, with plenty of satiny petals and feathery stamens that in many cases respond to touch and curl up before your eyes. Prickly pears are native as far north as New Jersey and the warmer parts of coastal Massachusetts and Connecticut. Once established, they grow on and on, and even in drought years will thrill the gardener with their golden blooms.

- There are two notable pachysandras, the Japanese (*Pachysandra terminalis*) and the American, often called Allegheny spurge (*P. procumbens*). The Japanese species grows up to a foot in height and is hardy as far north as USDA Zones 6 and 7, but in warmer areas makes a poor showing. It's an excellent— though unimaginative—groundcover. Low and stoloniferous stems are topped with circles of olive green leaves. They do well in shade and are best when planted so there's no room for weeds. White flowers with small petals appear in the spring. There is a cultivar called 'Variegata' with the leaves edged with white. Deer will usually pass this by unless very hungry.
- Believe it or not, Russian sage (*Perovskia atriplicifolia*) originally came from Afghanistan and Pakistan. It's a hardy perennial that reaches a height of up to five

feet, blooming with tall spikes of lavender flowers. Provide full sun and the plant is quite happy in dry to average soil. The square stems indicate membership in the mint family, and the scent might be the reason that deer do not immediately attack this plant.

- Ribbon grass or whistle grass (*Phalaris arundinacea*) is often found growing around abandoned farmhouses, as it was once a staple perennial for the floral border. The attractive leaves are striped with green and white. When held between joined thumbs and blown on by a kid, the blades make a shrieking, whistle-like noise. These grasses can be rampant when not held in check.

- New Zealand flax (*Phormium* spp.) is a member of the agave family and hails from New Zealand. These plants are tender perennials and not reliably hardy below USDA Zone 8, although they will overwinter in pots when kept dry and at about 40°F. The flowers, when they bloom, are interesting, but it's the leaves that make the display. The word *Phormium* is derived from *phormos*, meaning basket, and refers to the use of the leaf fiber for basket making and the commercial manufacture of ropes and twine. There are many cultivars available in attractive colors from green, yellow, and white, to red-purple and deep copper, often striped with yellow, orange-red, or salmon pink. The height ranges from three to fifteen feet, depending on the cultivar and the growing conditions. They make a great statement in my North Carolina garden

and are especially suited for coastal gardens. I suspect that deer resent the fibers.

- Balloon flowers (*Platycodon grandiflorus*) are a one-
species genus, originally from Japan where they are
often eaten, and from China where the dried roots
are a staple of herbal medicine. The unopened flowers resemble little hot air balloons. Plants often reach
a height of three to four feet and need to be tied up
to prevent flopping. There are a number of cultivars
of various colors available from catalogs.

- Jacob's ladder or Greek valerian (*Polemonium
caeruleum*) is a perennial wildflower from Europe and
Asia with subspecies native to America, generally the
West. Paired leaves grow from stems to three feet tall
and bear loose clusters of violet-blue bells in late
spring and early summer. Here is another plant utilized by Native Americans to treat all sorts of ailments, from snakebite to complications with the
bowels.

- Potentilla or cinquefoil (*Potentilla* spp.) are named
for the palmate leaves that number five. The flowers
are five-petalled and usually yellow when blooming in
spring. Most of the species have astringent roots that
were used by Native Americans to treat diarrhea. I
suspect that's why deer avoid the plants.

- Silver lace vine (*Polygonum aubertii*) is a rampant
climber that bears fleecy bunches of small, white
flowers in the summer and, when in full bloom, looks
like the froth on ocean waves. The stems are very

strong and quickly encircle most any support. The leaves are usually so thick a growing vine can substitute for an overhead canopy for protection from the sun. They are not fussy as to soil and adapt to full southern sun or partial shade.

- Primroses (*Primula* spp.) are charming flowers of spring with the common cowslip (*P. veris*) and the English primrose (*P. vulgaris*) being stars of the garden when there's shade and moist soil. The fragrant, five-petalled flowers come in many colors and arise from tufts of leaves that resemble lettuce. There is a mealy texture to the stems and unopened buds that apparently deer do not relish.

- Lungworts (*Pulmonaria* spp.) bear very pretty flowers of pink, white, or lavender in very early spring, and as flowers fade, produce rosettes of slightly hairy but very attractive leaves usually spotted with silver. They like moist soil and light to medium shade, and in areas with warm summers, often wilt. These plants are often mentioned in the "Doctrine of Signatures," where a plant that resembled a human organ (in this case, thanks to the spots, lung tissue) was thought to cure a disease afflicting that organ. While deer often leave these plants alone, my good garden friend, Allison Arnold, Director of Horticulture at the North Carolina Arboretum, reminded me that when times are hard deer will chew upon pulmonarias.

- Buttercups (*Ranunculus* spp.) are another one of those plants that, if rare, everybody would want a few of for the perennial border. The palmately-divided leaves grow on two- to three-foot stems and in spring produce many shiny, golden-yellow flowers that gleam on cloudy days or in early twilight. The fresh leaves and the poulticed roots were used by many Native Americans and early settlers to treat ailments like gout and skin abrasions. But be warned: The sap can cause intense pain and burning of the mouth. Yellow water buttercups (*R. flabellaris*) are aquatic plants with three-inch leaves divided into hair-like segments and bearing pretty, waxy-yellow blossoms about an inch wide.

- Goldenrods (*Solidago* spp.) are popular garden perennials in Europe, having been collected in America back in the 1700s. They are still commonly thought to be the source of fall hay fever, although ragweed has long been known as the true culprit. The cultivars make great garden subjects, especially as they bloom in late summer and early fall. A few were used in folk medicine, but some authorities believe that fungus-infected plants could be poisonous to the system. Regardless, their stiff stems are unpopular forage with deer.

- Common tansies or golden buttons (*Tanacetum vulgare*) are coarse, aromatic perennials that grow about three feet high and bear bunches of small, tubular, golden-yellow flowers. The dried leaves are used medicinally and the leaves have insecticidal properties. The oil from this plant is lethal and a half-ounce

can bring death within four hours. It's a charming
wild plant.

- Star jasmine or, as it's sometimes called, Confederate
  jasmine (*Tracheolospermum jasminoides*) is a twining
  vine or groundcover that reaches a length of up to
  twelve feet in a season. "Confederate" doesn't refer to
  the South but to the Confederated States of Malaysia.
  Small clusters of very fragrant, white, star-like flowers
  bloom in May and June. While only hardy to USDA
  Zones 8 and 9, I grow these vines in large pots
  (backed by a trellis), and they are moved into an un-
  heated potting shed with winter temperatures never
  below 40°F—and they do beautifully year after year.
  There is a dwarf form called 'Nana'. These plants
  need a fertile, high-moisture soil and partial shade,
  for in nature they are protected by a high tree canopy.
- In general, mulleins (*Verbascum* spp.) are plants that
  form basal rosettes consisting of gray-green leaves,
  usually having the texture of well-worn flannel, and
  tall stems with attractive, yellow flowers of small
  stature. The wild biennial known as the common
  flannel plant (*V. thapsus*) is naturalized throughout
  the Northeast and most of the Southeast. Its flower
  stalks are covered with the same tiny hairs that adorn
  the leaves, and I suspect the texture is not attractive
  to our hoofed friends. Although the common flannel
  has fewer flowers than the more cultivated types, it's
  a great plant for a desert or low-water garden and is
  quite attractive when planted in groups.

- Hungarian speedwell (*Veronica latifolia*) is a pubescent or hairy perennial, up to eighteen inches high, blooming during the summer months. Spikes of sky-blue flowers bloom over a long period, and if dead-headed will repeat the flowering. They are very attractive plants, and apparently deer dislike the hairs.

- It's a shame that deer find wisteria (*Wisteria* spp.) an unattractive food, as here's one vine that usually could benefit from some pruning. When left to its own devices, wisteria becomes rampant and, upon reaching a tree trunk of any girth, will eventually choke the plant to death. I have seen these vines actually twist steel poles. So vigilance is required when it comes to pruning. Nevertheless, when in bloom, they are spectacular plants.

- Yuccas (*Yucca* spp.) are large-scale American desert plants found in most of the country. They produce stiff, sword-shaped leaves up to four feet long, often tipped with a needle-like spine. Some species produce trunks with clusters of leaves at the top. They are beautiful landscape plants, great as living fences to keep dogs (and children) out of the garden area. In late spring to mid-summer, they produce tall spikes of beautiful, waxy-petalled flowers that open in the evening. The most common species for gardens are Adam's-needle (*Y. filamentosa*), soapweed (*Y. glauca*), mound-lily yucca (*Y. gloriosa*) with leaves growing from a short trunk, and Spanish bayonet

(*Y. aloifolia*) with a height to fifteen feet, a five-foot spread, and stiff, pointed leaves up to two and a half feet long. It's interesting to note that Native Americans once used yucca roots to make a powder which they sprinkled on still waters to put the fish beneath to sleep, causing them to rise to the surface.

## Bulbs to Brighten Up Spring

The following bulbs are resented, ignored, or nibbled at by deer in order to tweak gardeners. Remember, deer love crocuses (*Crocus* spp.) and tulips (*Tulipa* spp.), and will sometimes eat wood hyacinths (*Endymion* spp.). Also, my own garden experiences show that, although deer know that daffodils (*Narcissus* spp.) are poisonous to consume, they have been known to nip off the blossoms then toss them aside. Whether or not this is a veiled threat to the gardener, one never knows.

- Ornamental onions (*Allium* spp.) belong to the same genus that produces the common onion that serves as a garnish for hamburgers. Deer avoid all members of the onion family and, luckily, the following bulbs not only do beautifully in the average garden (as long as your clay soil is cut by enough humus to offer good drainage), but according to the species, also bloom in late spring and on into summer. The leaves disappear a few weeks after bloom is over. They bloom in many colors, including yellow, blue, pink, white, and purple, and with time increase in size. You should provide full sun, but they will tolerate some shade, especially down South. The cultivar 'Moly' blooms with an umbel of yellow, star-like flowers on foot-high stems. *A. christophii* or the Star of Persia is probably the most beautiful, with enormous, silver-purple flowerheads of hundreds of individual blossoms. 'Ivory Queen' is under eight inches, with wide leaves surrounding a white ball of small flowers. *A. giganteum* is a dramatic star with round, six-inch balls of deep purple blossoms on four-foot stems.

- Lily-of-the-Nile (*Agapanthus africanus*) are tender bulbs only hardy to USDA Zone 7 and then they must be mulched. Tropical plants can take far more cold than people imagine but resent damp, chilly temperatures, especially below 40°F. These lovely lilies boast many narrow, strap-like leaves and bear tall scapes topped with round umbels of funneled flowers, from twelve to thirty individuals, in pale lavender and light blue. As with many potted plants, provide some fertilizer during the growing season as continual waterings will deplete the earth's fertility. Remove flowers before seeds form.

- Mariposa lilies (*Calochortus gunnisonii*) demand perfect drainage, whether in the garden or in pots. Below USDA Zone 8, they must be mulched in the winter and cannot stand alternate freezing and thawing. The three-petalled flowers are banded from white to purple and edged with glandular hairs. These are absolutely beautiful flowers.

- Autumn crocuses or meadow saffron (*Colchicum autumnale*) are perennial flowers growing from corms native to Europe and North Africa. These are not to be confused with the regular spring crocus (*Crocus* spp.), a plant that deer are very fond of nibbling. In the U.S., these plants bloom in the fall, with lovely purple to white crocus-like flowers on short stems and without any leaves. The leaves appear in the spring. These plants are highly poisonous and used today for a gout treatment and, in the nursery industry, to double chromosomes in plants such as daylilies. Obviously, deer know the dangers.

- Winter aconites (*Eranthis hyemalis*) generally appear in late winter to early spring and carpet the ground with pretty, inch-wide, buttercup-like flowers of golden yellow. They warm a heart burdened by the cold and the snow. Attractive leaves persist as a groundcover until late spring, when they disappear from the scene after building up food reserves for bloom the next year.

- Fritillaria or frits (*Fritillaria imperialis*) produce spring flowers consisting of whorls of lance-shaped, light green leaves and umbels of three to six pendant, bell-shaped flowers in orange, yellow, or red. The flowers have a foxy smell that deer don't like, but it is not offensive to most people; you must put your nose up against the flowers to get more than just a hint. The other member of this tribe is called the checkered lily (*F. megaleris*), a smaller plant bearing single, nodding, bell-shaped flowers something like upside-down tulips. The petals are actually marked like part of a chessboard. Provide full sun to partial shade, moist soil, and let them alone after planting.

- Snowdrops (*Galanthus nivalis*) are very early blooming bulbs of great charm. Bulbs grow in bunches, each bulb sending up a one-flowered stem, the flower with three large petals and three that go almost unnoticed. When coming up, thick leaves protect the bud when pushing through the soil. Flowers remain open for a long time. With the coming of spring, the leaves disappear until the following year. They are not reliable in areas warmer than USDA Zone 7.

- Common hyacinths or Dutch hyacinths (*Hyacinthus orientalis*) are great spring flowers, reliably coming up year after year. Once the favored bulbs of the French, it was the Victorians who popularized growing the bulbs in special glasses using water as a medium. Dutch nurseries produced most of the colorful cultivars of today. Plant bulbs four inches deep and about three inches apart. Some people are allergic to the bulbs and get a skin reaction, which might explain deer not wanting to get their noses too near.

- Summer snowflakes (*Leucojum* spp.) are bulbous perennials with straplike leaves and nodding, dainty, white flowers. Despite their name, they usually bloom in late winter or early spring. The flowers are mildly fragrant with six petals (really three sepals and three petals) each with a green spot at its tip. 'Gravetye Giant' is larger than most of the species and the one usually offered by bulb dealers. Plants should be set out in bunches for greater effect. They like a good, well-drained soil but will tolerate clay soil, too.

- Tiger lilies (*Lilium lancefolium*) are tough and beautiful plants that grow for years in abandoned gardens. Originally from Asia, they arrived on our shores in the late 1700s. They're worth a try—none were ever eaten by deer in our New York garden, but that is no guarantee. Provide full sun and average garden soil.

- Grape hyacinths (*Muscari* spp.) are among the most popular bulbs of early spring. A genus of over thirty species, some come from the Mediterranean region and others from Asia Minor. Depending on the species, they bloom from early to late spring. Muscari are small bulbs. Plant them four inches deep and use a lot of them to make a big display. Full sun and reasonably drained soil are needed. The flowers set seed and will naturalize without being invasive.

- As noted above, daffodils (*Narcissus* spp.) are poisonous. They like heavy soils, naturalize with ease, and are available in many different sizes and flower forms. By choosing the proper cultivars, you can have blossoms from early spring right up to the end of May. Some of the best large cultivars are 'Fragrant Rose', with white petals and a rose-pink cup; 'Ice Follies', having white petals and a yellow cup; and

'Barrett Browning', with white petals and an orange-red cup. Three smaller cultivars are 'Thalia', with two to three white flowers on one stem; 'Chit Chat', a later-blooming flower on a six-inch stem; and 'February Gold', one of the best for late-winter bloom.

- Siberian squills (*Scilla siberica*) bloom in early spring, with vibrantly blue flowers of great charm. They deserve greater popularity, especially because they are not liked by deer and because they naturalize over your lawn with ease but disappear before mowing time. Squills bear up to ten star-shaped, blue-purple flowers, providing vibrant blues to your early spring grass. Pink and white cultivars are available.

- Death camas (*Zigadenus nuttalii*) are members of the lily family. Grass-like leaves grow from an onion-like bulb, followed by a leafless stem topped with a branching cluster of many greenish-white, star-like flowers, about a half-inch wide. It blooms in spring and is an attractive and interesting plant for the wildflower garden. A toxic alkaloid substance present in the entire plant causes breathing difficulties followed by a coma in humans, and also poisons grazing livestock, including deer.

## Ferns for that Shady Glen

Ferns are great additions to the garden, either as groundcovers or specimen plants. They prefer a good garden soil, partial shade (especially in the South), and plenty of water. If your space is limited, think about growing ferns in pots spread about the backyard—this gives the gardener more control over the fern's environment.

I suspect that the following list is incomplete, but deer have been documented as avoiding those ferns listed below. One reason for deer's aversion to many ferns could be that their various medicinal qualities lead to bad taste.

- Christmas fern (*Polystichum acrostichoides*) is a very attractive evergreen fern with spiny-toothed, holly-like leaflets, making it a popular holiday decoration. The fronds begin their first year growing erect, but as the seasons pass, they fall back to the ground, remaining for another year or two while new fronds emerge. While preferring a rich, limy soil, it will survive just about anywhere, sometimes in swamps and sometimes in rocky, open spaces. This fern grows about three feet high. Christmas ferns make an effective erosion control. This is a great plant for massing on slopes.
- Cinnamon fern (*Osmunda cinnamomea*) is large, coarse, common, and vigorous, with the arching fronds growing from a heavy rootstock covered with thickly matted horsehair-like roots. In late spring, golden cinnamon, club-like, fertile leaves arise from the clumps, easily distinguishing it from any other fern. It's the most common fern in the United States and found in almost every swamp, where large colonies form fern jungles. Their height can reach more than three feet. The matted rootstocks of the

*Osmunda* genus are often used as a growing medium for orchids.

- Royal fern (*Osmunda regalis*) reaches a height of over six feet, with translucent, pale green foliage, but it's quite delicate in its overall appearance. Royal fern is an inhabitant of wetlands and the edges of streams and will grow happily in a few feet of water, along the edge of a lake, and wet places in general. Because it grows from a crown rather than runners, this fern spreads slowly. Provide a cool, acidic soil. The leaflets turn golden-brown in the fall. Osmundas tolerate some sun if they have adequate moisture but do their best in light shade.

- Hay-scented fern or boulder fern (*Dennstaedtia punctilobula*) is a delicate, creeping plant with graceful fronds of a pleasant yellow-green. It prefers a dry, shaded site and is often found in hillside pastures. It rapidly spreads by crawling rootstocks and, once established, can invade many parts of the garden but is easily pulled up by hand. The fronds turn white when touched by frost. Plants are about sixteen inches tall.

- Interrupted fern (*Osmunda claytoniana*) is a reasonably large fern standing about four feet high. The arching blades have distinct interruptions in the center of the stem where sterile leaflets were. This makes them very easy to identify. One of the earliest ferns to appear in spring, it grows in most soils and prefers dry to wet spots.

- New York fern (*Thelypteris noveboracensis*) bears delicate, yellow-green fronds with three (or sometimes more) leaves per tuft and grows in spreading colonies without ever being a threat to neighbors. The leaves are about eighteen to twenty inches high and are found naturally at the edges of woodlands in reasonably dry soil. The leaves bleach out with frost.

- Ostrich ferns (*Matteuccia struthiopteris*) are one of the largest ferns in North America, reaching heights in excess of five feet. The gracefully arching leaves resemble ostrich plumes of a rich, dark green and lend an architectural quality to any garden. Although tropical in looks, they are exceptionally hardy, surviving winters to USDA Zone 3. Found growing along streams and riverbeds, they prefer plenty of water and a lot of sun. They wither with the first frost. Deer do not like this fern at all. Ostrich fern is not a good choice for the Deep South.

- Sword ferns (*Nephrolepis* spp.) are mostly tropical ferns from America, Africa, Malaysia, and the West Indies. The most popular variety of this fern is the well-known Boston fern (*N. exaltata bostoniensis*), with its long, drooping fronds and easy adaptation to a home environment. The most popular is *N. exalta*, found in Florida and California. These ferns need a temperature above 50°F. Deer do not like these ferns—if nothing else, you should grow some in pots for a dashing look to a backyard oasis.

- Sensitive or bead ferns (*Onoclea sensibilis*) reach a height of about two feet, with leaves unlike most other ferns because the blades are large and lack frilly indentations. There are prominent network-forming veins in the leaves. The common name, "sensitive," refers to their shriveling at the first frost. The second name, "bead fern," refers to the erect, beadlike, fertile spikes that over winter and were often used in dried flower arrangements. They do well in damp or wet places, in full sun or shade, and are quite attractive groundcovers.
- Bracken fern (*Pteridium aquilinum*) is probably the most common fern in the U.S. From three to six feet tall, the fronds are divided into three parts, each bearing triangular leaves, growing on stout stems, and making a very attractive groundcover. Although Native Americans and early settlers used various bracken mixtures to treat stomach cramps and diarrhea, and smoked fronds for headaches, the plant is poisonous in large doses. White-tailed deer will only eat small amounts in the summer or the fall, and generally avoid this fern. Goats are the only livestock that normally eat bracken. The fronds are thought to release hydrogen cyanide when they are bruised, and the taste is bitter.

## Shrubs and Trees

Once they have reached a certain height, shrubs and trees are fairly deer-proof. It's getting them there that's the problem. Until a tree or shrub or bush exceeds the browsing height of a deer (from three to five feet high), it's a good idea to protect it with a cage of chicken wire, snow-fencing, or a plastic tube with ventilation holes.

This section lists shrubs and trees that are ignored by deer, but there are others that deer make a beeline for. They include American arborvitae (*Thuja* spp.); balsam fir and Fraser fir (*Abies* spp.); Norway maple (*Acer* spp.); eastern red-buds (*Cercis* spp.); winged euonymus (*Euonymus alata*), itself a weedy and invasive plant; golden rain tree (*Koelreuteria* spp.); apples; cherries; plums; many rhododendrons (*Rhododendron* spp.); shrub roses; European mountain ash (*Sorbus* spp.); and the yews (*Taxus* spp.), though this last is confusing, as yews are poisonous to everything else.

- Catclaw (*Acacia greggii*) is a member of the mimosa family and also known as the Texas mimosa. It's a shrub that can reach tree stature and a height of about twenty feet, blooming with yellow flowers in spikes over two inches long. It is a well-armed plant that can be daunting to deer; they only eat new growth, so once you have a substantial plant started, you should be worry-free. Plants need plenty of sun and water and are only hardy to USDA Zone 9 and above.

- Japanese maples (*Acer palmatum*) are one of my favorite trees. Most of the Japanese maples I've grown have been cultured in pots on the terrace, so my knowledge of deer's eating habits with this particular plant is limited. I called Patricia Smyth of Mountain

Maples, located in Laytonville, California, and asked her about deer and maples.

"It's been our experience," she said, "that deer might take a leaf for a taste test, but then immediately move on to better pickings. When they are starving it's a different story, but when given a choice they ignore Japanese maples."

Japanese maples are incredibly beautiful trees ranging in height from a few feet to upwards of forty. There are over 200 cultivars of *A. palmatum*, plus other Asian maple species in the same league. Collecting these trees often turns into a lifelong pursuit. Japanese maples can easily be grown in pots and, when pot diameter is over a foot, they can overwinter outdoors in USDA Zone 7. One of the most beautiful is the laceleaf Japanese maple (*A. palmatum dissectum*), with such finely cut leaves that only a deer with 20/20 vision will ever spot them.

- The tree of heaven (*Ailanthus altissima*) is a prized tree in China, brought to America as a landscaping tree because it grows just about anywhere a seed lands (Betty Smith's book, *A Tree Grows in Brooklyn,* salutes that tree). It has become an outstanding weed tree and has invaded many parts of the country, choking out native species, but ironically deer will not touch it. And when all is said and done, it's an attractive tree in the landscape. Trees can reach a height of sixty feet and are very attractive when covered in flowers—but

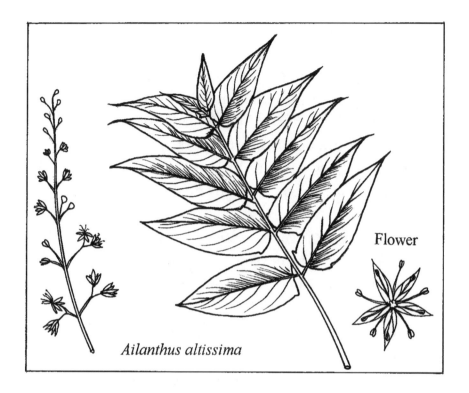

Flower

*Ailanthus altissima*

if choosing this tree, buy a female, as the male flowers emit a sweetish but fetid odor.

- Allegheny serviceberries or juneberries (*Amelanchier* spp.) are shrubs or small trees that live along the edges of woodlands in the Northeast, although *A. arborea* will do well down to northern Florida. I personally can vouch for this lovely tree because, every spring up in the Catskills, just about when you were ready to give up any hope that spring would arrive, up at the crest of the hill behind our farmhouse there would appear a burst of white flowers like a galaxy of stars. We knew then, even if the blossoms were blown by snow-laden winds, the wildflowers of May were not too far away. And in all those years of living there, despite the countless deer that walked on that hill, the serviceberries were never touched. But when the blooms turned to berries, that was a different story—and unless we were there when the ripening occurred, the birds never left a berry to find.

- False indigo (*Amorpha fruticosa*) is a native shrub that can reach twenty feet and resembles a small tree. The branches are woody and the twigs are hairy and green. Palmate leaves have 13 to 25 one- to two-inch leaflets dotted with resinous glands. The dark purple flowers are terminal, blooming in clustered spikes. Fruit is about a quarter-inch long and also bears resinous dots. Reliably hardy to the warmer parts of USDA Zone 5, false indigo has become somewhat invasive in wetlands, so care should be used in planting. While deer have been known to break branches, they apparently resent the resinous flavors. In spring, just remove the damaged wood.

- Japanese angelica (*Aralia elata*) is a shrub or a tree reaching a height of forty-five feet, with attractive, feathery leaves, and usually covered by spines. During spring, panicles of white flowers are followed by black fruits. When properly cooked, angelica is an edible mountain vegetable, but it contains saponins and alkaloids. Angelica has a long history in Korean traditional medicine; the bark and roots are used in treating cancer, diabetes, and gastritis. There is a cultivar bearing leaves with white margins called 'Variegata'. It's easy to grow and adapts to any well-drained soil in sun to light shade. This tree is also tolerant of city pollution and neglect.

- Monkey-puzzle trees (*Araucaria araucana*) are only hardy south of USDA Zone 7, but everybody who ever read an Agatha Christie mystery story should recognize the name. No matter what library, manor home, or vicarage a murder occurred in, there was always a monkey-puzzle tree in the garden. These evergreen, coniferous trees originated in Chile, where they are the most important coniferous timber crop. Monkey-puzzles are rather bizarre-looking trees, up to seventy feet high, growing in a loose, pyramidal shape, with stiff, scale-like leaves of dark green. The common name was bestowed by an Englishman in the 1800s who remarked that it was a puzzle as to how a monkey could climb such a tree. They do well in pots.

- For information about the hairy manzanita (*Arctostaphylos columbiana*), I spoke to Wallace W. Hansel of Native Plants of the Northwest in Salem, Oregon. According to Mr. Hansel, the hairy manzanita is one of the best native ornamental plants for the landscape in the Northwest. And deer, unless times are extremely tough, ignore the plant. It's one of the first plants to colonize an open canopied forest. It's a small, slow-growing evergreen shrub, from three to ten feet in height, with reddish-brown bark, and simple, blue-green leaves that are hairy on both sides, thus not that attractive to deer. Plants flower in spring with clusters of small, pale pink to white urn-shaped blossoms, followed by small, red fruits that look like tiny, flattened apples. Manzanita means "little apple" in Spanish.

- Ponytail palms (*Beaucarnea recurvata*) always had a place in all my gardens—but only growing in pots. In nature they are only hardy south of USDA Zone 9. With age these plants can reach a height of fifteen feet and are easily spotted because of their greatly swollen trunk base and the narrow, recurving, light green leaves. If your garden is warm enough, use these as specimen plants or grow them in a pot. They like a well-drained, sandy soil and full sun.

- Except for garden interest, barberries (*Berberis* spp.) are not a great group of plants to get a grip on. They have thorns up and down the bark and would seem to be unpleasant to eat. Wintergreen barberry (*B. julianae*) are great-looking shrubs, about four feet high and three feet wide, and impenetrable because of thorns. The foliage is a glossy, deep green and yellow flowers bloom in early April, followed by blue-black fruits. Mentor barberry (*B.* x *mentorensis*)are rounded and upright shrubs reaching a height of about six feet with a six-foot spread. The dark green leaves turn yellow to red in the fall. Yellow, waxy-petalled flowers appear in early spring, followed by a dull red fruit. When planted in a row, they form an impenetrable barrier or hedge. Japanese barberry (*B. thunbergii*) is a beautiful plant, growing about five feet high with a five-foot spread. Leaves are medium green, turning scarlet in the fall. Creamy white flowers are followed by orange-red fruits. Does well in poor soil and also forms an impenetrable hedge.

- Deer dislike at least three of the birch family (*Betula* spp.). The first is the paper birch (*B. papyrifera*), that tree of legend whose bark was used by Native Americans to make canoes; the second is the European white birch gray (*Betula pendula*), a smaller, short-lived tree to forty feet; and the third is the gray birch (*B. populifolia*), a tree of poor soil, short of stature, but with a very attractive, chalky bark. All three of these trees dislike warm temperatures and are best below USDA Zone 7. While they won't last long, they are most beautiful to look at and will grace yard or garden.

- Butterfly bushes (*Buddleia* spp.) are so popular with butterfly lovers that it seems strange nature didn't make them a deer treat just to be persnickety. This open and irregular-growing shrub can reach a height of seven to eight feet with a six-foot spread and, when in flower (usually most of the summer), it's a treat to both the eye and the nose; the fragrance of 'Black Knight' is reminiscent of an aged cherry cordial. They need full sun, good drainage, and a soil with good fertility, so it's necessary to fertilize every year or so. Most gardeners treat this shrub like a perennial and cut it to the ground in the fall.

- The common boxwood (*Buxus sempervirens*) fits the description of a compact shrub to a T. After all, it takes hundreds of years to reach thirty feet; like the oak, this is not a tree to plant for instant gratification. Hardy to USDA Zone 6, these dense shrubs with their lustrous, dark green foliage can be used in many landscapes—but perhaps the most important thing about this boxwood is its smell, especially on damp days. Boxwood leaves give off a strange fragrance, slightly foxy and penetrating but quite distinctive, liked by some and abhorred by others. Apparently, deer dislike the smell, too.

- Common catalpas or Indian bean trees (*Catalpa bignonioides*) are popular lawn and street trees, very showy when in bloom, and pendant with fifteen-inch-long bean pods in the fall. The common catalpa can reach a height of sixty feet and is often unmercifully cut back in city yards. The tree is ill-smelling when bruised, hence it is disliked by deer.

- Leatherleaf (*Chamaedaphne calyculata*) is a mostly perennial evergreen shrub with lily-of-the-valley-type blossoms and very tough and leathery leaves, sometimes red, not green, on the undersides. Plants begin blossoming just as snow is melting. A toxin called andromedotoxin is released if leaves are infused in boiling water. Notes from New Jersey point out that leatherleaf is a minor part of white-tailed deer's winter browse. Canadians report small amounts are consumed by caribou in Michigan and northern Canada. Leatherleaf does well in poorly drained sites or those with standing water, is acid-tolerant, and needs such conditions to multiply. A great bog plant.

- Bottlebrush (*Callistemon citrinus*) is a twelve-foot-high shrub, hardy north to USDA 8, consisting of three-inch-long, leathery leaves with a distinct scent of lemons (hence the species name). It's grown primarily for the floral display that consists of many bright red, three-inch spikes full of one-inch stamens, like bottlebrushes for small glassware. It's tolerant of soil, withstands drought, and is a good plant for beach-front properties.

- California lilacs or redroots (*Ceanothus* spp.) first came to my attention when touring the gardens of Sissinghurst, in southern England. Deciduous or evergreen shrubs, growing to small trees, one cultivar of *C. arboreus* from the Catalina Mountains of California has been reported as being reasonably deer-proof: 'Mills Glory' grows about three feet tall and bears bright blue flowers.

- Deodar cedar (*Cedrus deodar*) came to America from India, imported as a sterling addition to landscape planting. Reaching a height of about fifty feet, the tree exhibits a pyramidal shape with pendulous branches decked with one- to two-inch, bluish-green needles growing in dense bunches. Four-inch cones are rarely produced. Provide sun or partial shade in soil with reasonably good drainage. It is not hardy below USDA Zone 6.

- Golden cypress (*Chamaecyparis pisifera* 'Filifera') is a great conifer, an evergreen shrub or small tree six to eight feet high (if you wait a lifetime, it can grow to a height of fifty feet). The form is a broadly conical, loose, droopy mound like a large rag-mop, with thin, filament-like branchlets. The dwarf form, 'Filifera Nana', is better for the small garden. They are hardy to USDA Zone 4 and were imported from Japan back in 1861.

- The English hawthorn (*Crataegus laevigata*) will reach a height of twenty-five feet with a twenty-foot spread; it has attractive form and foliage, white flowers in spring followed by small red fruits, and sharp thorns. Hardy to USDA Zone 5, this is a great landscape plant and, if protected when young, will eventually provide its own defense.

- Chinese dogwood (*Cornus kousa*) is a large shrub or a small tree with dense, horizontal branching and lots of attractive leaves. Height is eventually fifteen feet with a ten-foot spread. It blooms later in the spring than the native dogwood (*C. florida*) and the pure white flowers are lovely. The species seems to be resistant to the dogwood anthracnose that attacks more wood-dwelling specimens. A red fruit appears in the fall. It's hardy to USDA Zone 6. While deer will look

for the native dogwood, they seem to leave this
species alone.

- The Leland cypress (x *Cupressocyparis leylandii*) is an
evergreen hybrid named for C. J. Leyland of Hagger-
ston Hall. It's a fast-growing cultivar, eventually getting
up to sixty feet and forming an upright, graceful pyra-
mid of soft, pointed leaves. Soft green when young,
this tree is dark blue-green and scaly when mature. It
is exceptionally tolerant of soil, asking only for moderate drainage and a mostly dry spot. The only pests
seem to be bag-worms. Deer seem to pass this one by.
- Japanese flowering quince (*Chaenomeles japonica*)
grows from three to four feet high with a three-foot
spread. Coarsely toothed leaves grow on spreading
branches and, in the spring, produce single, over one-
inch-wide flowers of white to red to orange, followed
in the fall by yellow fruits. It's a rapid grower and responds well to pruning. Provide sun or partial shade
in most any soil short of pure clay. This is a great
plant when it comes to withstanding city conditions
and, because the branches are very thorny (wear
gloves when pruning), deer generally pass it by.
- Daphne (*Daphne mezereum*) is a deciduous or semi-
evergreen shrub with simple leaves but, in the early
spring, incredibly fragrant flowers that bloom in a
spike, are white to lilac to rose-purple, followed by a
red or yellow drupe of fruit. Height is between four
and five feet. This is one beautiful plant and not to

be confused with the other winter daphne (*D. odora*). While glorious in the garden and not usually attractive to deer, this plant, and all parts of this plant, are poisonous. The plant or seeds can actually kill and often damage the retina.

- Russian olives (*Elaeagnus angustifolia*) can be weedy and, as such, are on the danger lists of many states. That said, they are attractive trees with small but very fragrant, creamy yellow flowers in spring, followed by small, yellow fruits with silvery scales. Their silvery-gray foliage is very attractive, and Russian olives always look much older than their calendar age, thus adding stature to a garden. They are rapid growers and will do well in poor soil. Remember, you want the variety with thorns, var. *spinosa*—it's the spines that do the trick.

- Enkianthus (*Enkianthus campanulatus*) is an upright, deciduous shrub that typically grows six to eight feet tall (less frequently to fifteen feet). Tiny, bell-shaped, creamy-yellow to whitish-pink flowers with pink striping and edging appear in pendulous clusters (racemes) in late spring. Individual flowers resemble those of Pieris, which is in the same family (heath). Elliptic, serrate, medium-green to bluish-green leaves (to three inches long) are crowded near the branch ends. Fall color is variable, but at its best features quality red foliage with tones of orange, yellow, and purple.

- Beech trees (*Fagus grandifolia*) are big and beautiful, making splendid specimens that cast a deep shade

beneath their broad, rounded crowns. At maturity
they can be sixty feet tall. Leaves are bright green
and turn golden-brown in the fall. The bark is a
smooth, light gray. Likes plenty of sun and a good
soil. Often found at the edge of a woods. They are
difficult to transplant, so buy either a potted plant or
one that has been professionally balled-and-
burlaped. Deer usually pass this tree by, so young
specimens can be easily protected with chicken wire.

- Forsythia (*Forsythia* spp.) are big, beautiful, and
blowsy shrubs well known for their spring display of
clear yellow flowers that cover the plant and brighten
any corner. Forsythias are very rapid growers and can
get quite overgrown if not pruned occasionally, most
effectively by cutting them to the ground every three
or four years. They grow in an upright but spreading
fountain of hollow stems; some stems get to be very
long and should be nipped off, something that deer
rarely do. Foliage turns reddish purple in fall. There
are a number of cultivars available.

- Dyer's broom (*Genista tinctoria*) is a small, shrubby
plant that, in my garden, is about two feet high and
thick with narrow pointed leaves. In May the plant is
covered with yellow, pea-like flowers of such color in-
tensity that toward twilight they almost light the border. The plants grow wild in Scotland and the hills of
England and sometimes along the edge of the road
in the Northeast. Bright green stems are streaked
with brown bark and respond beautifully to pruning.

The flowers are followed by inch-long pea pods. If cows eat Dyer's broom, their milk becomes bitter to the taste. I have never observed it being eaten by deer.

- At one time honey locusts (*Gleditsia triacanthos*) were grown for their wood, usually employed in making fence posts as it lasted a long time and resisted rot. It's also an excellent yard tree, eventually growing up to fifty feet high and having attractive feathery or pinnate compound leaves up to eighteen inches long, with each leaflet around an inch. They endure poor soil and put up with a lot of mistreatment. And they have formidable thorns that make pruning them somewhat of a misery. But a row of honey locust seedlings makes an attractive, and impenetrable, hedge. For the weak at heart, there is a thornless variety known as *G. triacanthos inermis*. To keep deer away, plant the old-fashioned kind with thorns.

- Rose-of-Sharon (*Hibiscus syriacus*) is a shrub or a small tree, fast-growing, doing well in moist soil and standing up to hot weather. Originally from China, this plant requires full sun to partial shade in the Deep South. There will be winterkill at the northern end of the range. Blossoms resemble mallows and appear in summer. This is a shrub that is grown for the flowers, so prune back in spring, leaving two to three buds on a stem. While old-fashioned plants are OK, I prefer 'Diana', one of the newer cultivars, because unlike the species, the beautiful white flowers stay open all night and the dark green foliage is more attractive. USDA Zone 5 is the bottom end for cold.

- When gardening in continually deer-infested Sullivan County, a number of plants escaped damage—one was a very old but vigorous Pee-Gee hydrangea (*Hydrangea paniculata* 'Grandiflora'). Pee-Gee simply refers to the initials of species and cultivar. The stems of a well-grown specimen of this shrub are strong enough to be used as walking-sticks. Eventually the shrub can become a tree up to twenty feet high. The flower clusters are often large enough to surprise garden visitors. This shrub is tolerant of soil and prefers partial shade.

- The hollies (*Ilex* spp.) are notable plants of great beauty. There are male and female plants, so you must have two sexes for fruit. A few are quite deer-resistant, including my favorite, a rather rare entry known as Perny holly (*I. Pernyi*). Originally from central China, this glorious plant has been at home in my garden for some fifteen years. This evergreen shrub has a height up to twelve feet with a six-foot spread, and alternate light green and shiny leaves with irregular spines. This irregularity here is the key: Deer cannot bite down and depend on working their way around regularly spaced thorns. Hardy from USDA Zones 6 through 9, tolerating sun or partial shade, this is one great shrub—when it's covered with more than the average showy red fruit, "spectacular" is the word to use. The native American holly

(*I. opaca*) is a tree to thirty feet high with a twenty-
foot spread. The leaves are dark green on top and
light green beneath. The small flower is white and the
fruit is a lovely red, especially when grown as a specimen plant. Deer often eat the berries, but unless
truly hungry will pass on the leaves. The inkberry (*I.
glabra*) is an evergreen shrub, about nine feet tall
with a seven-foot spread. The leaves are a shiny, dark
green, flowers are inconspicuous, and female plants
produce quarter-inch black berries in the late summer. Male plants have the best winter color. Provide
sun or shade, in a good garden soil. They are great
background plants and excellent for naturalizing.

NOTE: Even though its scientific name is *Ilex vom-
itoria*, the yaupon holly is a great tree to have for all
wildlife, including deer, who list it as a favorite
browse.

- Junipers (*Juniperus* spp.) are evergreens from many
parts of the Northern Hemisphere, including
North America and China. The leaves are needle-
like or scale-like, and many of the species produce
fragrant resins. They range in height from ground
crawlers to seventy-five feet. Junipers are also favorites for bonsai. Most junipers are deer-resistant,
a fact easily shown by the number of cedars (*J. virginiana*) growing along roads in the eastern part of
the United States. A favorite juniper is *J. chinensis*
var. *procumbens* 'Nana', a crawling shrub with
twisted and curving branches, prickly needles, and

the ability to fall over walls with graceful beauty. Sargent's juniper (*J. chinensis sargentii*) is another spreader, with a one-foot height and a spread of six to eight feet. And don't overlook the shore juniper (*J. conferta*), an evergreen of up to eighteen inches in height, with a six-foot spread. It tolerates low fertility and is excellent on beach dunes. Creeping juniper (*Juniperus horizontalis*) is another low-growing evergreen with needle-like foliage and blue berries in the fall. For years up in Sullivan County, we grew pfitzer junipers (*J. chinensis* 'Pfitzeriana') along the front of the house. Named for E. H. H. Pfitzer of Germany, these shrubs grow about seven feet high with a spread of up to ten feet. The foliage is bright green and scale-like. Tolerant of soil, these plants prefer full sun—and be warned, they do get very large, so don't plant them in front of a foundation. They grow fairly fast and are great for carpeting a bank.

- Mountain laurels (*Kalmia latifolia*) are large and robust shrubs, with bright green evergreen leaves and mounds of glorious and interesting white to deep rose flowers in spring. With age, they can become gnarled and beautiful trees. Shade or sun, they do best in partial shade on well-drained, even rocky, soil. There are a number of cultivars available, usually varying by flower size and color. Sheep or pig laurel (*K. angustifolia*) only reaches a height of three feet and often covers mountainsides from the Catskill

Mountains right down the Appalachian chain. The leaves are poisonous and generally left alone by deer.

- Japanese rose (*Kerria japonica*) represents one species of deciduous shrub with slender stems and sparse, thin, light green foliage. Flowers are yellow, bloom in early spring, and resemble a small rose. The plants reach a six-foot height and a five-foot spread. The hollow stems are small in diameter and almost as tough as bamboo. They are tolerant of poor soil but prefer good drainage.

- A well-grown beauty bush (*Kolkwitzia amabilis*) is a thing of beauty, for in early May the six- to seven-foot branches, with a spread of seven feet, are festooned with pink, tubular flowers with yellow throats. The cultivar 'Rosea' has larger flowers. Kolkwitzias bloom in profuse clusters. The gray-green leaves turn a reddish color in the fall; the plant has no pest problems and makes a great shrub border. They do not transplant well, so buy potted or professionally balled-and-burlaped plants. Because these shrubs bloom on old wood, prune after bloom, taking no more than one-third of the wood in a year. The bark on older stems exfoliates, bringing winter interest to the garden. Hardy to USDA Zone 6.

- The golden chain tree (*Laburnum anagyroides*) is a small tree with dark green leaves, and in spring, pendant sprays of bright yellow flowers, obviously members of the pea family. Native to Europe, it's widely grown in North America as a specimen lawn tree.

Reaching a thirty-foot height, with a fifteen-foot spread, the only requirements are sun and well-drained soil. In fact, this tree does well on rocky slopes. But the leaves and the pods that follow the flowers are highly poisonous and some care should be taken. There is a hybrid (*L.* x *Watereri*) that is shorter than the species. This is the soft-limbed tree that is used to make a living arch in English gardens, an arch of joined trunks that then drip those pendant sprays of glorious flowers in late spring, making the cover of every garden magazine.

- We had a European larch (*Larix deciduas*) growing just above our driveway in our Cochecton garden, about twenty-five feet from a tall, old white pine (*Pinus strobes*), with its bottom branches making such a wide circle I always needed help to prop up those branches when cutting the lawn beneath. It sat there for twenty years and was never touched by the deer. Being a larch might have had something to do with its being spared—as the species name indicates, this is a deciduous tree that drops its needles in the fall, after they've turned a beautiful golden tan. So, about the time that deer are looking for browse, all the needles have fallen, with naught left but bare branches. Various extension agents say that the European larch is occasionally badly damaged by deer but it's more often left alone. Here's a lawn tree that's worth the effort.
- In all my woods wanderings in North Carolina, I've yet to see any dog hobble (*Leucothoe* spp.) that has

been stripped by deer. But one species, known as the drooping leucothoe (*L. fontanesiana*), is known by gardeners to be generally spared by deer. It's a graceful evergreen shrub between three and four feet high with up to a six-foot spread, demanding at least partial shade, and with arching stems boasting leathery leaves between three and five inches long. The plant likes a reasonable stab at drainage but otherwise will adapt to most soil conditions on the acid side. In early spring, two- to three-inch sprays of fragrant, white, waxy flowers attract early-rising bees. Pruning involves removing three-year-old canes to promote new growth from the crown. There is a beautiful cultivar known as 'Girard's Rainbow', bearing new leaves with colors of white, pink, and copper. It's hardy from USDA Zones 6 to 9, but resents excessive heat.

- Privets (*Ligustrum* spp.) are the hedge champions of all time, and clippers have been trimming them in North America since they were brought over from Europe (*L. vulgare*) in the 1700s, and from Japan, then China, in the middle of the 1800s and even the 1900s. Unfortunately, from the point of view of native plant specialists, the privets are bad news, as their dense thickets soon crowd out indigenous species. But gardeners can use this to keep deer at bay. When left to their own devices, privets can grow to a height of twelve feet with a ten-foot spread. The lustrous, dark green leaves are quite beautiful, not to mention the clusters of small, white flowers, followed by dark

purple fruits. This genus does very well in adverse
conditions, including city gardens. Occasionally, they
will be browsed by hungry deer, but unlike many
shrubs, privets respond to this pruning by sprouting
new branches.

- There are hundreds of species of holly grapes (*Mahonia* spp.), but high on the gardener's list is the
species from the American Northwest, specifically
the Oregon grape (*M. aquifolium*). These are evergreen shrubs growing to a height of ten feet, but usually around seven. Often leggy, we prune our
mahonias with purpose once every three or four
years. Alternate leaves are stiff and leathery, with
spines along the margins. Bright yellow, waxy,
scented flowers that reveal the plant's relationship
with barberries bloom in early spring. The fruits of
summer are blue-black, resembling elongated grapes
and favored by birds. Provide partial or full shade in
reasonably moist, well-drained acid soil. Hardy to
USDA Zone 6. While deer will occasionally attack
these shrubs (thus saving you the trouble), for many
seasons they are left alone. Native Americans used
this mahonia to treat a number of diseases, and recently scientists have found that herbal extracts from
mahonia can be useful in treating psoriasis.

- Heavenly bamboos (*Nadina* spp.) are neither heavenly nor bamboos, but earthbound members of the
barberry family. Due to a fine lacy foliage, its common name comes from a resemblance to bamboo

and the cane-like growth pattern of the stems. *Nandina domestica* is classified as an evergreen but will lose its foliage if the temperature drops below 10°F. The canes will die back to the ground at −10°F, but will come back readily the next spring. This plant provides color in the garden throughout the year. In the spring, the new foliage emerges as bright, bronzed red, and is soon followed by large, six- to twelve-inch panicles of creamy white flowers. As the season changes, the foliage becomes blue-green, fading to light green. Clusters of bright green berries replace the flowers. By late summer, the berries ripen to a bright red. In the fall, the foliage again begins to change to shades of pink and red, ending the year with bright red leaves and berries. The berries will remain until they are discovered and enjoyed by the local birds. Heavenly bamboo will slowly grow to eight feet if it is left alone; however, it can be kept at a very compact size by pruning. It is also suitable for growing indoors as a container plant. Nandina flowers attract bees, while the berries attract birds. The berries are possibly toxic to cats. Shorten or remove old canes to the ground; do not shear.

- Oleander (*Nerium oleander*) is a poisonous plant. All parts of the plant are harmful, including the sap. At one time this plant was featured in many mystery books; a single leaf has been known to be lethal. Even skin contact can cause a rash. That said, oleander is a fast-growing evergreen shrub, up to twenty feet tall and spreading about ten feet. Lance-shaped, leathery leaves average about six inches long. Fragrant summertime flowers are white, pink, red, salmon-pink, or a light yellow. Shrubs should be pruned to keep a good silhouette. Oleanders have a high salt and wind tolerance and so make excellent shore shrubs—plus they are drought resistant. They also do beautifully in pots. Hardy to USDA Zone 7 but must be protected or mulched in the winter. They do best in Zones 8 and 9.

- The spruces (*Picea* spp.) are represented in the deer-dislike list by the Colorado blue spruce (*P. pungens*), the species name referring to its sharp, pointed needles. Reaching a majestic height of seventy to ninety feet, this spruce is a great specimen tree. Provide good soil with good drainage and full sun. There are many cultivars available, including a number of dwarf conifers for the small garden. The Norway spruce (*P. abies*) can grow up to one hundred feet tall and spread up to thirty feet. These trees transplant with ease when professional balled-and-burlaped specimens are used. There are many smaller cultivars available. According to the USDA, Norway spruce nursery stock is not recommended when white-tailed deer are involved.

- There are two andromedas of note: Japanese andromeda (*Pieris japonica*) and mountain andromeda (*P. floribunda*). Japanese andromeda grows about six feet tall with a six-foot spread. The leaves are a lustrous, dark green and, in late winter to early spring, the flower buds that have graced the plant since fall begin to open. They bloom with waxy white, five-inch-long, pendulous clusters of great beauty. There are many cultivars. Hardy from USDA Zones 5 to 8. Mountain andromeda grows to about the same height and has the same flowering, but it's the hardier of the two, wintering over (with protection) to USDA Zone 5. The annual growth rate for these shrubs is less than one foot. Flowers are sometimes injured by heavy late frost. Provide a moist, acid soil in partial shade. Lacebugs can stipple leaf surfaces with tiny wounds, making them yellow and unsightly.

• Austrian pines (*Pinus nigra*) are listed by many sources as being disliked by deer. But according to USDA records, during a bad snowstorm in Wyoming, a herd of mule deer gained entrance to a conifer tree nursery where they browsed Austrian pine in preference to ponderosa pine (*P. ponderosa*), blue spruce (*Picea pungens*), bristle cone pine (*P. aristata*), and Rocky Mountain juniper (*Juniperus scopulorum*). Damage was concentrated on the lateral branch buds and needles. We had a number of Scotch pine (*Pinus sylvestris*) on our Cochecton property and, except for one year in the 1980s when ice storms ravaged the mountains, deer ignored them. Scotch pine can reach a height of seventy feet with a thirty-foot spread. Beautiful trees with dark green needles, they transplant well and are somewhat adaptable to soil, but need full sun. They are rapid growers compared to many evergreens, and useful as a specimen or in masses. According to the USDA, white-tailed deer will browse Scotch pine, but compared to other ornamentals, this species is low on the whitetail list. Red pine (*P. resinosa*) grows to seventy feet, has an attractive bark, does well in colder areas (below USDA Zone 6), and makes a good specimen or accent tree. If preferred food is lacking, white-tailed deer, snowshoe hares, and cottontails will browse red pine seedlings.

- Hardy orange (*Poncirus trifoliate*) is a fascinating shrub, hardy to USDA Zone 6, and ornamental all through the year. Glossy green leaves turn yellow in the fall and grow from low-branching stems that are adorned with heavy thorns up to four inches long. April flowers are waxy white, fragrant, and followed by yellow-orange fruits like small oranges. Eventual height is about fifteen feet with a twelve-foot spread. Will put up with city conditions and does well even in dry, infertile soils. When planted in a row, these shrubs make an impenetrable barrier because of their vicious thorns. 'Flying Dragon' has twisted stems and sharply curved thorns.

- Staghorn sumac (*Rhus typhina*) is one of my favorite shrubs for the small, or even the large, garden.

Highway departments hate it but horticulturalists love it. The Royal Horticultural Society gave this small tree three awards in the 1900s. This is another plant growing in our Cochecton garden that was never touched by the deer. The USDA reports that white-tailed deer and moose browse the leaves and twigs, while the bark and twigs are eaten by rabbits, especially in winter. But it's such a fast grower that deer browse never seemed to cut back any trees in the back field (and I always protect the trunks of any tree in my garden from rabbits). Alternate, feather-like compound leaves up to two feet long bear eleven to thirty-one leaflets and turn brilliant oranges and reds in the fall—more than enough reason for growing these beauties. The brown branches are velvety-hairy, resembling deer antlers. Maroon flowers are borne in upright panicles up to eight inches long. In the growing season, this small tree or shrub looks completely tropical. In winter, when leaves fall, the mature fruits remain on the twigs, making for a great silhouette. Use this plant for holding steep slopes, or mass them in places where other plants fight to survive. 'Laciniata' is a beautiful cultivar with many-cut leaves.

- Corkscrew willow (*Salix matsudana* 'Tortuosa') is a cultivar introduced to the U.S. in 1923 when the Arnold Arboretum received a cutting from China. By the mid-1930s, the tree entered hort-commerce, taking the flower arrangers by the throat—once

seen in a vase, everybody wanted it. My experience
with the beautiful specimen tree shows the typical
height to be about thirty feet. The alternate leaves
are simple, lanceolate, between two and four inches
long, bright green above and glaucous beneath.
When young, the stems are yellow, turning olive-
green, then brownish-gray with age. The contor-
tions are always impressive. The fact that deer seem
to ignore this tree is quite surprising but perhaps,
again, it's not the shape but the chemical content
which deters them.

- Common lilacs (*Syringa vulgaris*) bloom by the cottage door and, throughout the Northeast, are often
  found in abandoned gardens on derelict farms. The
  lilac isn't even a native to North America but actually
  came from Turkey in the sixteenth century, but it's
  the state flower of New Hampshire, where it was first
  imported in 1690. Everybody knows the flowers of
  lilacs, but to grow them to perfection, these shrubs
  require full sun, except when grown in the Deep
  South. They prefer a slightly acid soil. Most lilacs also
  require at least six weeks of below-40°F temperatures
  during the winter months. If that doesn't fit your bill,
  grow one of the 'Descanso' hybrids. After blooming,
  remove dead flowers to prevent seed formation.
  Every few years, just remove the oldest stems, cutting
  back to the ground.

- Leatherleaf viburnum (*Viburnum rhytidophyllum*) belongs to the honeysuckle family, grows as a shrub up

to ten feet tall, and has great architectural character. Up to seven inches long, the leaves are narrowly oblong, evergreen, conspicuously wrinkled, scruffy and thick, and dark green above while paler (and slightly hairy) beneath. Showy clusters of small, white flowers appear in May—but you grow this shrub for the leaves and the red, then black, berries of fall (you need two plants for berries). This shrub grows fast, prefers partial shade, and it tolerates an alkaline soil. The cultivar 'Allegheny' has abundant flowers. Hardy to USDA Zones 6 to 8 but suffers from the heat in warmer climates.

# 8

# *Lions and Tigers and Voles*

Some gardeners might think that grouping two big-time carnivores with the lowly mole might be an overstatement—let me quickly state that in many years of gardening, next to deer, the mole is said to be the cause of the most damage. And never has a poor creature suffered from so much bad press.

## *Good Times Underground!*

Last year when the snows of winter melted, gardeners in the colder parts of the country were confronted by a wealth of damage to plants caused by voles—that's right, voles, not moles.

This year another loud cry of despair was heard echoing from hill to hill, as everyone went out to the backyard and found their once-even lawns traversed with tunnels dug by moles—and an occasional shrew—and resembling the B & O Railroad Yards more than a swath of peaceful green.

The last few years have been some of the worst mole years on record. One way you can tell is by those tunnels; but another is by reading garden writers who attack these poor creatures in print as though they were furry drones sent by enemy nations to destroy the American way of life. Instead of trying a little understanding, we build better mole-death machines: from irritating them with Tabasco Sauce and chili powder to gassing them with carbon monoxide (messy to the lawn and dangerous to everybody).

And the surfeit of moles is always accompanied by a bumper crop of grubs, especially Japanese beetles.

Moles are little mammals with tiny eyes, small and virtually concealed ears, and very pretty, soft, iridescent fur. They live almost entirely underground, feeding on smaller animal life, especially earthworms and grubs. I repeat: Moles do not eat bulbs or roots. They will chew through them if the plants are in the way, but they do not ingest the results of their chewing. They are generally beneficial to gardens, especially when it comes to consuming vast numbers of vociferous grubs. I do admit that in their zeal to devour they often do some damage—by heaving up the soil, causing the grass to dry out quickly, and creating unsightly ridges or tunnel-tops, a sight that irritates some people more than paying taxes.

There are many methods used to remove moles, but outside cyanide gas—dangerous to both mole and man—nothing is sure. Catalogs sell windmills with spikes in the ground supposed to make a rumbling noise in the earth, scaring them away, but I've never seen it work; they still dig tunnels and hunt for food, moving out of the area only to dine.

Recently a garden writer suggested either putting a dead mole or a hunk of odoriferous cheese in the tunnels, but he has no proof that works either. And he gave no hint how to obtain a dead mole to begin with (although steel traps are offered for sale in some catalogs).

Poison bait isn't such a good idea, especially if you have a cat, dog, or child. But there is an effective biological control called milky spore disease that inoculates soil with a fungus that infects the grubs but bothers nothing else. The problem with this product is the time it takes to effect the cure: at least a year.

So before going out and putting a toxic waste dump in your backyard to do away with the little pests, or driving up the family car to gas them out, think ahead to next July and the damage the beetles will do to the garden. The number of moles is in direct proportion to the food supply—if your backyard and garden have a surfeit of moles, they probably need them.

Instead, buy a pair of those plastic shoes with spikes used to aerate the lawn (not, as someone thought, to kill the moles) and walk over those tunnels. Then plant some

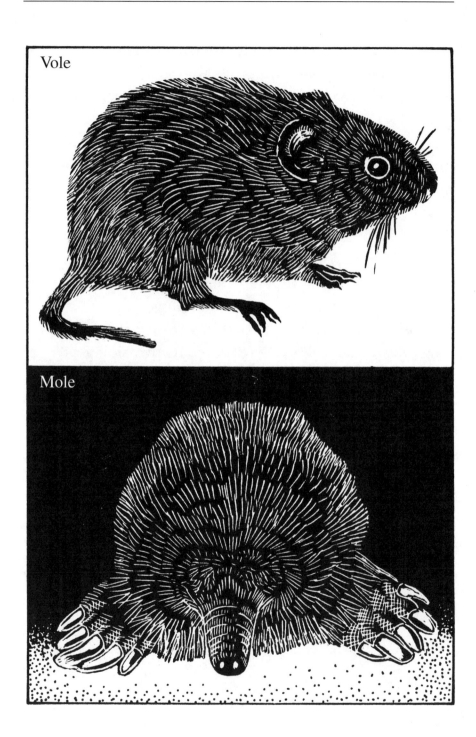

Vole

Mole

grass seed, rake it up a bit, and by mid-May you'll never know they were there.

## *Voles: On to the Big Time*

After deer, your worst garden enemy remains the vole. I went out into the garden last spring on one of the colder days to check on the damages wrought by weeks of ice and chill, coupled with the wind's bitter blasts.

Most plants survived, but the worst chlorophyllic assault by far was perpetrated by our little furry friend, the vole. Everywhere I turned, the litter on the ground, the hay mulches, the backyard lawn, and forgotten piles of leaves, were tunneled through and through. Where grasses touched the trunks of small trees and bushes such as my arctic willow or my Himalayan honeysuckle, the bark was chewed unmercifully. My entire line of lavender was eaten right down to soil level and, blast them!, they had taken all the leaves of the lamb's tongue and ripped them up for nesting material.

*The Complete Guide to American Wildlife* has this to say about the vole:

> Voles are best known to many readers by the popular name of "meadow mice." Voles have long, grayish brown fur, short ears and tails, and beady eyes. Their tails are more than an inch long and are not brightly colored. They live on the ground, usually in grassy terrain, where they make inch-wide runways, leaving

behind cut grass stems, and are active at all hours. They can swim and dive. In winter they make round holes to the surface through the snow. Their voice is a high-pitched squeak. They eat grass, roots, bark, and seeds. They construct a nest of plant material on the ground, and there are usually five to seven young.

There are a number of vole species, but the meadow vole (*Microtus pennsylvanicus*) covers the country out to the Mountain Time Zone, skipping the Deep South, while the long-tailed vole (*M. longicaudus*) goes from the Rockies to the Pacific, and the prairie vole (*M. ochrogaster*) joins these two areas in the center. In the South we have the pine vole (*M. pinetorum*).

The vole that did the damage to our gardens this year is the meadow vole, North Carolina being the southernmost state of their kingdom. They are between three and five inches long with an average two-inch tail. A population of fifteen to an acre can increase to 250 voles in four years, and obviously that kind of growth explosion has occurred in the land around our home.

Our garden cat, Miss Jekyll, has tried to do her bit with the vole menace. Every afternoon, a freshly killed subject turns up on the doormat, and I'm sure there are many more that she has dispatched out in the garden over the years.

Gardening in the mountains is never that easy, but the first trip to the garden this spring was the worst I've yet experienced. On the other side of the coin, the snowdrops were truly beautiful and the crocus the best yet. And by mid-June, with the exuberance of summer, the vole was a faint remembrance of things past.

## Fighting Voles

Do not stick a garden hose (or a hose hooked up to a car's exhaust) down a hole, because it's futile. And unless you live alone with no friends, no family, no pets, and no neighborhood attachments, do not use poison bait, no matter how attractive it appears.

Probably the safest method to protect valuable bulbs and expensive cultivars is to enclose bulb or root within a hardware cloth cage.

Other easy things to do in the war on voles include eliminating weeds, tall grasses (alive or dead), and all sorts of plant litter from the garden. Also, protect young trees by encircling the trunks with quarter-inch hardware cloth or plastic guards made especially for such purposes. For voles, make sure the barriers extend at least three inches below the ground and eighteen inches above the surface.

You can help your lawn by close-mowing in the fall before snows arrive, then raking up the cut grass.

Remember to be on friendly terms with local predators, including shrews (they are carnivores and always hungry), foxes, owls, bobcats (if you're lucky enough to have them), and, of course, snakes of all kinds. (This is another reason never to use poison in the garden.)

Next, you can try to install a barrier between the voles and their targets. There is a product on the market called VoleBloc, advertised as being safe, non-toxic, lightweight, and permanent. It's made from a kiln-fired, lightweight aggregate. According to Chuck Friedrich, RLA, the inventor of VoleBloc, to protect existing plants, use a garden fork or spade to dig a four-inch-wide, one-foot-deep "moat" around the drip-line of the plant. The drip-line is where drops of water would hit the ground from the most extended leaves. After the "moat" has been dug, fill it with VoleBloc to the top. Voles also like to tunnel under mulch, so it's best to reduce the mulch around the plant and use VoleBloc to mulch inside the moat instead.

For new plantings, after tilling the beds, make the planting hole twelve inches wider and two inches deeper than the root ball. Place two inches of VoleBloc in the hole. Then set the root ball on top of the VoleBloc and backfill around the roots with 100-percent VoleBloc, completely surrounding the roots. Mulch with VoleBloc around the stem.

For bulbs, place two inches of VoleBloc in the hole and place the bulbs, then surround them with VoleBloc, leaving just the tips exposed. Finally, place a fifty-fifty Vole-Bloc/soil mix over the bulbs to the desired depth. Don't worry about daffodils because they are poisonous to voles.

For more information, call toll free: (877) 737–6284; or visit the Web site: www.volebloc.com

Vole Repellents

As mentioned before, stay away from poisons—but there are a few repellents you might try.

Capsaicin is mentioned in Chapter Six. It's a harmless hot sauce used to protect ornamental trees and shrubs, fruit trees, fruit bushes, grape vines, and nursery stock from vole damage. Don't use it directly on food to be harvested.

Predator odors made from the urine of foxes and coyotes may be effective vole repellents. They are listed beginning on page 110.

Get a garden cat. Cats are effective vole hunters and often leave them as gifts at the doorsteps of appreciative owners.

Finally, you can use mouse snap traps for small vole populations, baiting the traps with peanut butter (it's amazing how peanut butter is a favorite of almost all living things).

## *The Lowly Cottontail*

There are hares and rabbits. They both belong to the genus *Lepus,* but species differ and, as a rule, hares and jackrabbits are larger and have longer ears and hind legs than cottontails.

Hares, for example, do not make a nest. After a thirty-some-day gestation period, three to eight young are born furred, eyes open, and able to move about within minutes.

We will overlook the arctic hare and just pause to mention the white-tailed jackrabbit (*Lepus townsendii*), an inhabitant of the Far Midwest; the snowshoe rabbit (*L. americanus*), which inhabits most of Canada and just the most northern part of the U.S.; the European hare (*L. europaeus*), making the area around the Great Lakes their home; and the black-tailed jackrabbit (*L. californicus*), a resident of the Southwest.

But when it comes to the cottontail, we enter the more populous areas of Pest City.

Cottontails are smaller than hares, have shorter ears and hind legs, and usually hide when threatened. Female cottontails breed at nine months of age and produce several litters a year. After about a thirty-day gestation period, about four or five helpless, naked, and blind young are born in a fur-lined nest in the ground. In less than three weeks, they are weaned.

These rabbits are small, with a sixteen-inch body and three-inch ears. Their fur is a grayish-brown, with the underside of the tail cotton-white, along with whitish feet. They live to about five years old.

Cottontails are found near farms, fencerows, junk piles, thickets, woodlands, or just about anyplace they can find both food and cover. They will even live in abandoned woodchuck holes. In spring and fall, they make a home called a *form,* a nest-like cavity made of grassy humps on top of the ground.

In our neighborhood in Asheville, some of the cottontails are so brazen as to chow down in the middle of a driveway while the folks who live there are out shopping. They can dine in early morning, early afternoon, or on into the night. They eat a lot of green plant material, damaging annuals, perennials, vegetables, and trees and shrubs. The last two succumb to a process called *girdling,* in which the rabbits gnaw around the trunk, successfully killing the tree by preventing the flow of water and nutrients from the roots to the rest of the plant. Rabbit damage includes gnawed or cleanly severed stems, plus their distinctive round droppings—and of course, in winter, their obvious tracks.

## Rabbit Control

For all the reasons mentioned before, do not try to poison rabbits. Instead, protect tree and shrub trunks from rabbits by encircling the trunks with quarter-inch hardware cloth or plastic guards made especially for such protection. You can also stack up proper-sized plastic planting pots with the bottoms removed, then cut down the sides. Make sure at least a couple of inches are under the ground and the tops are at least eighteen inches up the trunk.

Some people recommend mothballs—but I suspect this cure is worse than the disease.

Instead, try removing all those thickets where rabbits can hide. Clean up brush heaps, infested weed patches, litter piles—in fact, anyplace a rabbit can hide.

Think about getting a dog, too—or a cat.

Refer to Chapter Six for repellents that are effective against rabbits, including predator urines.

Small-mesh chicken wire can be very effective around a garden plot, or in eighteen- to twenty-four-inch cylinders around young trunks. Small units can be set around precious perennials.

Havahart traps are very effective when used to trap rabbits. Bait them with fresh greens, oats, apple chunks, even cat kibble. Move them around to different locations if you aren't catching anything.

## How Much Wood Can a Woodchuck Chuck?

Woodchucks or common groundhogs (*Marmota monax*) are familiar animals of the roadside. There, all summer long, they can be seen eating greens in preparation for the coming winter. Amazingly, they are members of the squirrel family, and count among close relatives prairie dogs, flying squirrels, and chipmunks.

They are large animals, up to two feet in length (sometimes a bit larger), with little ears; short, powerful legs; and a medium-long, bushy, and somewhat flattened tail. The fur is dark brown to yellowish brown above and a paler, sometimes rusty color below. Older woodchucks get gray hairs, too. They can weigh up to fourteen pounds, especially after eating all summer. They usually waddle rather than actually walk, but they can move very fast. They can also climb and swim. And when disturbed they make their presence known with a sharp whistle.

Woodchucks live along the edges of open land and along fencerows, grass-covered gullies, and stream banks. Here, in the sides of banks or under existing walls, they dig their burrows. The main entrance is usually located near a tree stump and is hard to miss because of the pile of freshly excavated earth (in our case, the entrance was under a wall, with the soil helping the woodchucks to clamber over the top). Side entrances are smaller and better concealed. The total amount of subsoil removed in the course of digging one burrow can total 700 pounds.

By the end of October, most woodchucks are hibernating in their underground nests. They usually sleep all winter, although during longer periods of mild weather some 'chucks may awaken and go outside.

Breeding begins in early spring, when a litter of two to nine naked, blind, and helpless kits is born.

The woodchuck occupies an important niche in the wildlife community: Skunks, foxes, weasels, opossums, and rabbits all use woodchuck burrows for their dens. Also, because tremendous quantities of subsoil are moved in the course of burrow construction, woodchucks contribute much to the aeration and mixing of the soil. Woodchucks are one of the few large mammals who venture out in daylight, and many people get enjoyment from seeing them.

When we lived in Sullivan County, we found that, along with deer and rabbits, woodchucks are a populous pest. They are almost total vegetarians, enjoying leaves, flowers, grasses, and, of all things, dahlias. When living near farms, they enjoy alfalfa, clover, and all sorts of truck-garden veggies. We were amazed to learn that they can climb trees or fences—so never place your vegetable garden close to a tree and, if fenced, electrify. (Being an excellent shot, up in the mountains I dispatched any that got too close.)

I never thought I would be confronted with woodchucks in Asheville, but this past spring I was not only host to a bonded pair, but two small (and cute) kits, as well. I spent a great deal of time down in the garden, accompanied by a friend's BB gun—within a week I only had the elder male to confront, as the rest of the family dispersed.

A neighbor told me that this particular woodchuck had been seen in the neighborhood for years, and judging by his many gray hairs, he was certainly not a young sprout. He usually lived back along an abandoned road just down the street from our yard and garden, but during the drought, I had the best greens around.

Here in the city we cannot shoot and poison is an absolute no, so the answer was a Havahart trap. Once trapped, we took the captured animal to a nearby wildlife center, which carried the animal out to the hills beyond.

## The Wonderful Chipmunk

There are two chipmunk species: the eastern chipmunk (*Tamias striatus*) and the western or least chipmunk (*Eutamias minimus*). Between them they take care of most of the eastern United States and much of the West, on up into Canada. Chipmunks are marvelous creatures—intelligent, clever, and well-groomed (they rarely have fleas or parasites). They can live as long as eight years, probably a bit longer when raised as pets.

The eastern chipmunk is about five or six inches long, reddish-brown above, white below, with stripes on its back and sides ending at the reddish rump. They have internal cheek pouches they can stuff with nuts and other foodstuffs.

Chippers live at the forest's edge, around rock piles, under or next to stone walls, in outbuildings, even in abandoned drain holes for tumbling walls. They are at home throughout the suburbs. They are not social and, except for mating, live happily alone in their tidy burrows. They are often seen sitting upright, looking over the lay of the land, giving out with a clear, repeated *chip* or a soft *chuck*. When startled, they sound out with several chips in a row, followed by a trill, then raise their tails in the air and quickly run to safety.

The least chipmunk is smaller, with yellowish or reddish fur, with stripes on its back and sides extending to the base of the tail.

Chipmunks eat nuts, berries, seeds, and insects, including earthworms, slugs, and grubs. They do not attack gardens with a vengeance, but many people think they do. They do not eat bulbs and pick them from your garden. Beyond some documentation of their eating (or storing) wild trout lilies (*Erythronium* spp.), the reports of chipmunk bulb vandalism are apocryphal. Chipmunk problems revolve entirely around the digging of burrows and movement of dirt.

If you feel threatened by chipmunks, the easiest solution is to get a cat.

I, on the other hand, have learned to fight back. Whenever I find the beginnings of a hole, I quickly fill it in, packing the dirt as tightly as I can. When the hole is renewed, I fill it again. Because chipmunks are intelligent and quite willing at a certain point to take their ease, they will eventually move if given enough prodding.

If you are interested in making a garden friend out of a garden foe, read *Eastern Chipmunks: Secrets of Their Solitary Lives* by Lawrence Wishner (Washington, D.C.: Smithsonian Press, 1982).

# Appendix 1

## *Deer-Resistant Plants for California*

Iasked my old garden friend, writer Joe Seals, about a list of deer-resistant plants for California's Central Coast. This is a large area, usually USDA Zones 8 and 9, and in many respects would also apply to the coastal parts of Texas, Louisiana, Florida, and on up into Georgia and South Carolina. He provided it, but added the following caveat: "After completing it from various 'deer-resistant' nursery lists and extension services, I went out to check some actual gardens where deer had visited. There were plenty of plants on this list that the deer had snacked on—obviously, they didn't read the list."

## Deer-Resistant Plants for California's Central Coast

### Trees

Acacia
Acer palmatum
Aesculus californica
Afrocarpus (Podocarpus)*
Agonis flexuosa
Albizia
Araucaria
Arbutus 'Marina'
Callistemon viminalis
Calocedrus decurrens*
Cedrus
Ceratonia siliqua
Cercis
Chiranthofremontia
Cupressus
Eriobotrya
Ficus
Fraxinus
Fremontodendron

Gingko biloba
Laurus nobilis*
Liquidambar
Lophostemon confertus
Magnolia
Maytenus boaria
Melaleuca*
Michelia doltsopa
Michelia x foggii
Olea europaea
Palms
Pinus
Podocarpus macrophyllus*
Quercus
Sciadopitys verticillata
Sequoia sempervirens
Tristaniopsis laurina
Umbellularia californica*
* can be hedged.

### Shrubs

Abelia x grandiflora
Acacia*
Alyogyne huegellii
Anisodontea

Arbutus unedo*
Arctostaphylos*
Artemisia
Banksia

*Buddleja*
*Buxus**
*Callistemon**
*Calycanthus*
*Carpenteria californica*
*Ceanothus* 'Concha'
*Ceanothus* 'Dark Star'
*Ceanothus* 'Julia Phelps'
*Chaenomeles*
*Choisya ternata*
*Cistus*
*Coleonema*
*Convolvulus cneorum*
*Coprosma**
*Corokia cotoneaster*
*Correa*
*Cotoneaster*
*Dendromecon*
*Dodonaea viscosa**
*Echium candicans*
*Erica*
*Eriogonum*
*Escallonia**
*Euryops*
*Fatsia*
*Feijoa**
*Fremontodendron*
*Garrya elliptica*
*Grevillea**

*Hakea suaveolens*
*Halimiocistus*
*Helimium lasianthum*
*Heteromeles arbutifolia*
*Ilex**
*Juniperus**
*Kerria japonica*
*Lantana*
*Lavandula**
*Lavatera assurgentiflora*
*Lavatera maritima*
*Lavatera thuringiaca*
*Leonotis ocymifolia*
*Leptospermum**
*Leucadendron*
*Ligustrum**
*Mahonia*
*Melaleuca**
*Michelia figo*
*Mimulus*
*Miscanthus*
*Myoporum**
*Myrica californica**
*Myrsine africana**
*Myrtus communis**
*Nandina domestica*
*Nerium oleander**
*Philadelphus*
*Plumbago auriculata*

*Pyracantha*
*Rhamnus californica\**
*Rhus*
*Ribes*
*Rosmarinus officinalis\**
*Salvia greggii*
*Sarcococca*
*Solanum rantonettii*
*Sollya heterophylla*

*Spiraea*
*Tecoma capensis\**
*Teucrium*
*Tibouchina urvilleana*
*Trichostemma lanatum*
*Vaccinum ovatum\**
*Viburnum\**
*Westringia fruticosa*
\* can be hedged

## Groundcovers

*Ajuga*
*Aptenia cordifolia*
*Arctotheca calendula*
*Armeria*
*Artemisia stellerana*
*Bougainvillea*
*Campanula poscharsky*
*Carex flacca*
*Ceanothus gloriosus*
*Ceanothus hearstiorum*
*Cephalophyllum*
*Cerastium tomentosum*
*Ceratostigma plumbag.*
*Coprosma* x *kirkii*
*Dymondia margaretae*
*Erigeron karvinskyanus*

*Erodium reichardii*
*Festuca californica*
*Festuca glauca*
*Festuca idahoensis*
*Fragaria chiloensis*
*Gazania*
*Geranium* 'Frances Grat'
*Geranium incanum*
*Hedera helix*
*Lampranthus*
*Myoporum* 'Pacifica'
*Myoporum parviflorum*
*Osteospermum*
*Persicaria capitata*
*Rosmarinus offic. prost.*
*Scaevola*

*Sollya heterophylla*
*Stachys byzantinus* 'Silver
  Carpet'
*Thymus*

*Verbena*
*Vinca*
*Zauschneria*

## Vines

*Bougainvillea*
*Gelsemium sempervirens*
*Hedera helix*
*Hibbertia scandens*
*Jasminum*

*Mandevilla (Dipladenia)*
*Solanum jasminoides*
*Tecoma capensis*
*Wisteria*

## Perennials

*Acanthus mollis*
*Achillea*
*Agapanthus*
*Agastache*
*Agave*
*Aloe*
*Arctotis*
*Argyranthemum Armeria*
*Artemisia*
*Bergenia*
*Brachyscome*
*Campanula poscharsky*
*Carex*
*Centranthus ruber*

*Centaurea*
*Convolvulus sabatius*
*Coreopsis*
*Dietes*
*Digitalis*
*Erigeron glaucus*
*Erigeron karvinskyanus*
*Erysimum*
*Euphorbia*
*Felicia amelloides*
*Ferns*
*Festuca californica*
*Festuca glauca*
*Festuca idahoensis*

*Geranium*

*Helleborus*

*Hemerocallis*

*Heuchera*

*Iris*

*Kniphofia*

*Leonotis*

*Limonium*

*Liriope*

*Lithodora diffusa*

*Muehlenbergia*

*Narcissus*

*Nepeta*

*Nierembergia*

*Ophiopogon*

*Origanum*

*Osteospermum*

*Pennisetum setaceum*

*Penstemon*

*Phlomis*

*Phormium*

*Romneya coulteri*

*Santolina*

*Scabiosa*

*Scaevola*

*Senecio viravira*

*Sisyrinchium*

*Stachys byzantina*

*Stipa*

*Tagetes lemmonii*

*Thymus*

*Tulbaghia*

*Verbena*

*Yucca*

*Zantedeschia*

*Zauschneria*

## Bulbs

*Allium*

*Amaryllis*

*Begonia*

*Colchicum*

*Crocosmia*

*Cyclamen*

*Dahlia*

*Freesia*

*Iris*

*Ixia*

*Leucojum*

*Narcissus*

*Scilla*

*Zephyranthes*

## Annuals

**Winter/Spring annuals:**

*Calendula*
*Campanula medium*
*Clarkia amoena whitneyi*
*Cynoglossum amabile*
*Lobularia maritima*

*Myosotis sylvatica*
*Papaver rhoeas*
*Scabiosa atropurpurea*
*Pericallis (Senecio)*
   x *Hybridus*

**Summer/Fall annuals:**

*Ageratum*
*Catharanthus roseus*
*Cleome hasslerana*
*Euphorbia marginata*

*Impatiens*
*Ricinus communis*
*Salvia farinacea*
*Tagetes patula*

# Appendix 2

## *Wildlife and Conservation Agencies in the United States*

If you have some free time at a computer—one with reasonably fast downloading—you can see for yourself just how big and full of hope this country is. The following Web sites will give you an idea of the great species distribution in the United States. And, foremost in the artwork of almost every site, you will find an antlered deer.

- U.S. Fish and Wildlife Service
  www.fws.gov
- Alabama Fish and Game
  www.dcnr.state.al.us/agfd
- Alaska Fish and Game
  www.admin.adfg.state.ak.us/license
- Arizona Game and Fish
  www.gf.state.az.us

- Arkansas Game and Fish
  www.agfc.state.ar.us
- California Fish and Game
  www.dfg.ca.gov
- Colorado Division of Wildlife
  wildlife.state.co.us/hunt
- Connecticut Department of the Environment
  dep.state.ct.us
- Delaware Department of Natural Resources
  www.dnrec.state.de.us/fandw.htm
- Florida Game and Fresh Water Fish
  floridaconservation.org
- Georgia Department of Natural Resources
  www.dnr.state.ga.us
- Conservation Council of Hawaii
  www.conservation-hawaii.org
- Idaho Department of Fish and Game
  www2.state.id.us/fishgame/fishgame.html
- Illinois Department of Conservation
  dnr.state.il.us
- Indiana Department of Natural Resources
  www.in.gov/dnr
- Iowa Department of Natural Resources
  www.state.ia.us/government/dnr
- Kansas Department of Wildlife and Parks
  www.kdwp.state.ks.us
- Kentucky Department of Fish and Wildlife Resources
  www.kdfwr.state.ky.us

- Louisiana Department of Wildlife
  www.wlf.state.la.us
- Maine Department of Natural Resources
  www.state.me.us/doc/index.html
- Maryland Department of Natural Resources
  www.dnr.state.md.us/index.asp
- Massachusetts Division of Fisheries and Wildlife
  www.state.ma.us/dfwele/dfw
- Michigan Department of Natural Resources
  www.michigan.gov/dnr
- Minnesota Department of Natural Resources
  www.dnr.state.mn.us/index.html
- Mississippi Department of Wildlife Conservation
  www.mdwfp.com
- Missouri Department of Conservation
  www.conservation.state.mo.us
- Montana Department of Fish, Wildlife, and Parks
  www.fwp.state.mt.us
- Nebraska Game and Parks Commission
  www.ngpc.state.ne.us/flashintro.html
- Nevada Department of Conservation and Natural Resources Division of Wildlife
  www.state.nv.us/cnr
- New Hampshire Fish and Game
  www.wildlife.state.nh.us
- New Jersey Department of Fish and Wildlife
  www.state.nj.us/dep/fgw
- New Mexico Department of Game and Fish
  fwie.fw.vt.edu/states/links.htm

- New York State Department of Environmental Conservation
  www.dec.state.ny.us
- North Carolina Wildlife Resources Commission
  www.wildlife.state.nc.us
- North Dakota Game and Fish
  www.state.nd.us/gnf
- Ohio Department of Natural Resources
  www.dnr.state.oh.us
- Oklahoma Conservation Commission
  www.okcc.state.ok.us
- Oregon Department of Fish and Wildlife
  www.dfw.state.or.us
- Pennsylvania Department of Conservation
  www.dcnr.state.pa.us/hometext.htm
- Rhode Island Department of Environmental Management
  www.state.ri.us/dem
- South Carolina Department of Natural Resources
  water.dnr.state.sc.us
- South Dakota Department of Game, Fish, and Parks
  www.siouxfalls.com/details.cfm
- Tennessee Wildlife Resources Agency
  www.state.tn.us/twra
- Texas Parks and Wildlife
  www.tpwd.state.tx.us
- Utah Division of Wildlife Resources
  www.wildlife.utah.gov/index.jsp

- Vermont Department of Fish and Wildlife
  www.anr.state.vt.us/fw/fwhome
- Virginia Department of Game and Inland Fisheries
  www.dgif.state.va.us
- Washington Department of Fish and Wildlife
  www.wa.gov/wdfw
- West Virginia Wildlife Resources Department
  www.dnr.state.wv.us
- Wisconsin Department of Natural Resources
  www.dnr.state.wi.us
- Wyoming Department of Game and Fish
  gf.state.wy.us

# Appendix 3

## *Deer Depredation Permits*

O n March 16, 2001, the following bill was referred to the Natural Resources Committee of the Iowa General Assembly. Known as House File 503, it deals with the issuance of deer depredation permits to landowners who have sustained deer-related damage. It's included here for readers in other states who would like a little background on the process.

PAG LIN
1   1   Section 1. <u>NEW SECTION</u>. 481C.4 DEER DEPREDATION PERMITS
1   2   – FEES – RESTRICTIONS – PENALTY.
1   3     1. Notwithstanding section 481C.2, a landowner who incurs
1   4   crop or nursery damage caused by deer population may apply to
1   5   the county recorder for not more than ten deer depredation
1   6   permits for each farm unit of eighty acres where the damage
1   7   has occurred. The department shall specify, by rule, a
1   8   proportional number of permits which may be issued for farm
1   9   units based on the size of the farm unit, damage done, and
1   10   deer population. The application shall specify the crops or
1   11   nursery stock damaged, the estimated amount of damage, and the

| 1 | 12 | area of the farm unit where the damage occurred. Each |
|---|----|---|
| 1 | 13 | application shall also be accompanied by a fee of twenty-five |
| 1 | 14 | dollars for each deer depredation permit requested. The |
| 1 | 15 | permit is valid only from September 1 through the succeeding |
| 1 | 16 | March 1 for taking a deer of either sex on the farm unit |
| 1 | 17 | specified on the application. If additional deer depredation |
| 1 | 18 | damage occurs after ten deer have been taken on a farm unit, |
| 1 | 19 | not more than ten additional depredation permits may be issued |
| 1 | 20 | with the approval of a representative of the department for |
| 1 | 21 | the same fee for each permit. A postcard shall be issued with |
| 1 | 22 | each depredation permit. A person taking a deer with the |
| 1 | 23 | depredation permit shall complete and return the postcard to |
| 1 | 24 | the county recorder within ten days after taking the deer. An |
| 1 | 25 | unused depredation permit and postcard shall be returned to |
| 1 | 26 | the county recorder by March 10 following the expiration of |
| 1 | 27 | the depredation permit. |
| 1 | 28 | 2. A landowner who has been issued a deer depredation |
| 1 | 29 | permit pursuant to subsection 1 may sell or give the deer |
| 1 | 30 | depredation permit to hunt on the specified farm unit to any |
| 1 | 31 | person who is otherwise licensed, except for a deer license, |
| 1 | 32 | to hunt in this state. If a deer depredation permit is used |
| 1 | 33 | by any person other than the landowner, the name and address |
| 1 | 34 | of the user shall be legibly written on the permit and on the |
| 1 | 35 | return postcard. |
| 2 | 1 | 3. Except during a regular shotgun season, any bow and |
| 2 | 2 | arrow or any legal firearm may be used to take a deer with a |
| 2 | 3 | deer depredation permit. |
| 2 | 4 | 4. A person who violates this section or a rule adopted |
| 2 | 5 | under this section is guilty of a simple misdemeanor which is |
| 2 | 6 | punishable as a scheduled violation under section 805.8, |
| 2 | 7 | subsection 5, paragraph "e". |
| 2 | 8 | Sec. 2. Section 805.8, subsection 5, paragraph e, Code |
| 2 | 9 | 2001, is amended to read as follows: |
| 2 | 10 | e. For violations of sections 481A.85, 481A.93, 481A.95, |
| 2 | 11 | 481A.120, 481A.137, 481B.5, 481C.4, 482.3, 482.9, 482.15, and |
| 2 | 12 | 483A.42, the scheduled fine is one hundred dollars. |
| 2 | 13 | EXPLANATION |
| 2 | 14 | This bill authorizes the owner of a farm unit which has |
| 2 | 15 | incurred crop or nursery damage caused by deer population to |
| 2 | 16 | apply to the county recorder for not more than 10 deer |
| 2 | 17 | depredation permits for each farm unit of 80 acres where the |
| 2 | 18 | damage has occurred. The department shall specify, by rule, a |

| 2 | 19 | proportional number of depredation permits which may be issued |
|---|----|---|
| 2 | 20 | for farm units of varying size. The application shall specify |
| 2 | 21 | the crops or nursery stock damaged, the estimated amount of |
| 2 | 22 | damage, and the area of the farm unit where the damage |
| 2 | 23 | occurred. Each application shall be accompanied by a fee of |
| 2 | 24 | $25 for each depredation permit requested. Each depredation |
| 2 | 25 | permit is valid only from September 1 through the succeeding |
| 2 | 26 | March 1 for taking a deer of either sex on the farm unit |
| 2 | 27 | specified on the permit. If additional damage occurs after 10 |
| 2 | 28 | deer have been taken on a farm unit, not more than 10 |
| 2 | 29 | additional depredation permits may be issued with the approval |
| 2 | 30 | of a representative of the department of natural resources for |
| 2 | 31 | the same fee. A postcard shall be issued with each |
| 2 | 32 | depredation permit which shall be completed and returned by |
| 2 | 33 | the hunter within 10 days after taking a deer. An unused |
| 2 | 34 | depredation permit and postcard shall be returned to the |
| 2 | 35 | county recorder by March 10. |
| 3 | 1 | A landowner who has been issued a deer depredation permit |
| 3 | 2 | may sell or give the permit to hunt on the landowner's farm |
| 3 | 3 | unit to any person who is otherwise licensed, except for a |
| 3 | 4 | deer license, to hunt in this state. If a deer depredation |
| 3 | 5 | permit is used by any person other than the owner of the farm |
| 3 | 6 | unit, the name and address of the user shall be legibly |
| 3 | 7 | written on the permit and on the return postcard. |
| 3 | 8 | Except during a regular shotgun season, any bow and arrow |
| 3 | 9 | or other legal firearm may be used to take deer with a deer |
| 3 | 10 | depredation permit. |
| 3 | 11 | A person violating the provisions of this section is guilty |
| 3 | 12 | of a simple misdemeanor, which is punishable by a scheduled |
| 3 | 13 | fine of $100. |
| 3 | 14 | LSB 3108YH 79 |
| 3 | 15 | tj/gg/8 |

# Index

236